ROUTLEDGE LIBRARY EDITIONS: CONSERVATION

Volume 2

INTERNATIONAL TRADE IN WILDLIFE

INTERNATIONAL TRADE IN WILDLIFE

TIM INSKIPP AND SUE WELLS

NEW YORK AND LONDON

First published in 1979 by IIED, London

This edition first published in 2020
by Routledge
52 Vanderbilt Avenue, New York, NY 10017

and by Routledge
2 Park Square, Milton Park, Abingdon, Oxon OX14 4RN

Routledge is an imprint of the Taylor & Francis Group, an informa business

© 1979 Earthscan

All rights reserved. No part of this book may be reprinted or reproduced or utilised in any form or by any electronic, mechanical, or other means, now known or hereafter invented, including photocopying and recording, or in any information storage or retrieval system, without permission in writing from the publishers.

Trademark notice: Product or corporate names may be trademarks or registered trademarks, and are used only for identification and explanation without intent to infringe.

British Library Cataloguing in Publication Data
A catalogue record for this book is available from the British Library

ISBN: 978-0-367-43303-1 (Set)
ISBN: 978-1-00-300237-6 (Set) (ebk)
ISBN: 978-0-367-40873-2 (Volume 2) (hbk)
ISBN: 978-0-367-80994-2 (Volume 2) (ebk)

Publisher's Note
The publisher has gone to great lengths to ensure the quality of this reprint but points out that some imperfections in the original copies may be apparent.

Disclaimer
The publisher has made every effort to trace copyright holders and would welcome correspondence from those they have been unable to trace.

INTERNATIONAL TRADE IN WILDLIFE

CITES - the Convention on International Trade in Endangered Species of Wild Fauna and Flora - was signed in Washington DC in March 1973, and entered into force in July 1975.

By the time of the second conference of the parties, held in San José, Costa Rica, in March 1979, 51 states were members of CITES.

CITES prohibits international commercial trade in the rarest 600 or so species of animals and plants, and requires licences from the country of origin for exports of about another 200 groups.

Wildlife is big business. One shipment into the United States can be worth a million dollars. A fur coat from South American ocelots sells for $40,000 in Germany. A single orchid or Amazonian parrot can fetch $5,000. Rhinoceros horn is worth more than its weight in gold.

Third World nations need the support of CITES to prevent poaching and smuggling, and to reinforce their national policies. But some of the main wildlife-importing countries are still not members of the convention - Japan, Belgium and Italy, for example.

Is the objective of CITES to work towards the total abolition of international trade in wildlife? Or is it to regulate the trade so that a regular, sustainable wildlife crop can be taken, even of such animals as elephants, monkeys, whales and cheetahs?

What is the role of zoos, butterfly collectors, animal dealers? Can turtles, crocodiles and other wildlife be farmed? Who pays for implementing the CITES convention? How do the wildlife merchants evade the customs controls? Are all the CITES nations really trying to enforce it?

This briefing document includes the full text of the CITES convention; lists all the animals and plants controlled by CITES; describes the latest decisions of CITES taken in Costa Rica and Bonn, 1979; and gives a detailed background to the current international traffic in monkeys, spotted cats, whales, ivory, parrots, tortoises, marine turtles, crocodiles, butterflies, sponges and rare orchids.

CHAPTER 1 INTRODUCTION	3
Early legislation	4
The international trade	5
CITES: the first moves	6
The Washington Convention	6
CHAPTER 2 WHAT DOES THE WASHINGTON CONVENTION SAY?	10
CITES parties	13
CHAPTER 3 THE SECRETARIAT	
Who pays?	15
Observers and NGOs	16
The role of IUCN and the SSC	16
Red Data Books; TRAFFIC	17
CHAPTER 4 HOW IS CITES ENFORCED - AND HOW EVADED?	
Forms and permits	18
Customs and identification	19
Tourism; disposal of confiscated specimens	20
National reports	21
The European Economic Community	21
Stockpiling; transit trade and laundering	23
Sanctions	26
How recognisable is a product?	27
CHAPTER 5 THE WILDLIFE TRADE	
Overview	27
The CITES appendices	30
Marsupials and monotremes; primates	31
Whales and dolphins: the IWC	36
The international fur trade: spotted cats and others	39
Seals	43
Wolves and bears	46
Otters; elephants and ivory	47
Skins, horn, wool, musk	51
Birds	54
Amphibians and reptiles: dying pets and turtle soup	59
Reptiles: towards crocodile farms	65
Fish; molluscs	70
Butterflies: the Taiwan connection	72
Sponges: a case for action?	74
Plants: cacti and succulents	75
CHAPTER 6 SECOND CITES CONFERENCE: COSTA RICA, 1979	78
Finance; changes to the appendices	80
ANNEX 1 THE TEXT OF THE CONVENTION	83
ANNEX 2 APPENDICES I, II AND III	89
READING LIST	103

ISBN No 0-905347-11-0

Published by IIED, London

Printed by House of Print
D'Arblay St, London W1

© Earthscan 1979

CHAPTER 1   INTRODUCTION

- Of approximately 13,200 mammal and bird species estimated to be living in 1600, over 130 have already become extinct. About 240 more are today in danger of extinction.

- Large numbers of reptiles, amphibians, fish and invertebrates are also endangered, and there are an estimated 20,000-25,000 endangered plants.

- Three quarters of these species have become extinct or endangered as a direct result of man's activities - especially hunting and habitat destruction.

- There is a long list of animals extinct as a result of direct exploitation, including:

  * the quagga
  * Steller's sea cow
  * the West Indian monk seal
  * the great auk (a flightless penguin-like bird from the subarctic)
  * the Falkland wolf
  * the sea mink
  * the Carolina parakeet
  * the passenger pigeon
  * several Galapagos and Indian Ocean giant tortoises

- The passenger pigeon is a good example. In the early 1800s it ranged so abundantly throughout the USA that it was hunted by the million for the commercial meat market. By the 1850s it was noticeably less common, but the hunting continued. In one 40-day period in 1869 nearly 12 million pigeons were sent to market from Hartford, Michigan, alone. The last wild passenger pigeon was shot in 1908. The last captive one died in a zoo in 1914.

- During the 20th century there has been a slow realisation that hunting and exploitation of wildlife would have to be controlled. Wildlife is a finite resource, which has to be managed if a continuous supply is required.

- This realisation had been appreciated by earlier civilisations. The Incas of Peru (13th-16th centuries) had very effective management techniques to ensure the conservation of the vicuña, a deer-like animal related to the llama, which was an important natural resource for meat, skins and wool. The vicuña was sacred, and killing it without permission a state offence. The government regulated its hunting, which took place at intervals, in restricted areas and at limited seasons. Animals from which the wool was sheared were released back into the wild. With the fall of the Inca Empire after the Spanish Conquest, this management plan was abandoned, and vicuñas were killed indiscriminately.

Early legislation

- Some of the earliest recent wildlife management legislation also relates to the vicuñas. In 1825 the liberator Simon Bolivar issued a decree prohibiting the killing of the vicuña in Peru. Unfortunately, the market for vicuña products ensured that the killing continued, and it was not until a protection agreement between Bolivia and Peru in 1969 that the decline was halted. As a result of strict protection, numbers have recovered.

- In the USA in the 1890s it became clear that commercial hunting and the consequent trade in wild meats and wildlife products had to be controlled. In 1900 the Lacey Act was passed, which outlawed interstate traffic in birds and mammals that had been taken illegally in their state of origin. In 1913 the Wilson Tariff Act ended imports into the USA of wild bird plumes for women's hats.

- The Lacey Act was later amended to prohibit the import of all wildlife killed, captured or exported illegally from its country of origin. This was the first instance of one nation's laws supplementing the wildlife protection of others.

- In other countries early wildlife legislation was concerned with welfare (eg the UK Cruelty to Animals Act 1876), the control of agricultural pests (eg the UK Destructive Imported Animals Act 1932), the control of hunting and the taking of trophies (eg the Wild Animals and Birds Protection Enactment 1925 of the Federated Malay States, the Ugandan Game Ordinance 1926 and the Kenyan Game Ordinance 1937) and the setting up of national parks and game reserves (eg the Kenya National Parks Ordinance 1945 and the 1926 act founding the Kruger National Park in South Africa); the early legislation concerning national parks did little except ensure that European colonists could get their hunting trophies.

First wildlife conventions

- One of the earliest international wildlife agreements was the 1911 Fur Seal Convention between Russia, Japan, the UK (on behalf of Canada) and the USA.

- Indiscriminate hunting had reduced the fur seals of the Pribilof Islands (west of Alaska) from two million to just over 100,000. Under the convention, only the USA was allowed to hunt the seals. The other countries received compensation, calculated as a percentage of the annual revenue from the seals.

- Other international conventions and treaties followed: the London Convention for the Protection of African Fauna and Flora in 1933, and the convention between the USA and other American republics on Nature Protection and Wildlife Preservation in the Western Hemisphere in 1942.

- In 1946 the International Convention on the Regulation of Whaling was concluded. It is hard to consider this a conservation treaty since it has allowed gross overhunting and presided over the steady decline of whale numbers.

- In spite of national and international legislation, the pressure on wildlife from man has continued to increase - perhaps not surprisingly, when the population of many tropical countries is doubling in less than 25 years.

The international trade

- Commercial trade in wildlife centres primarily on its products: meat, fur, feathers, hides and scales. But live animals have been increasingly exploited. In 1925 there were about 125 zoos in the world, mainly in Europe and North America. Since the 1950s there has been a dramatic increase in numbers. In 1976 there were 981 zoos and aquaria listed in the International Zoo Yearbook. In the UK the number of zoos has increased from 14 in 1945 to over 80 in 1976. The countries with most zoos are the US, UK, China, Japan, East and West Germany and the USSR.

- The developing countries of Asia, Africa and Latin America are net producers of wildlife. The wealthy, industrialised nations of Europe, North America, Japan and elsewhere are wildlife consumers.

- Producer countries can make large amounts of money out of their wildlife. As it becomes rare, the market value increases. Thailand for example, was an important producer of wildlife from the 1950s until the mid 1970s; exports reached a peak in 1970. In 1974 there were 200 animal dealers in Thailand, 20 of whom were specifically licensed to export wildlife.

- During 1967 and 1968, 547,000 birds, 31,000 mammals, and 42,000 reptiles and amphibians were traded in Thailand for a value of $1.9 million. Exports equalled 38% of the volume of this trade and 87% of the value, so the trade continued even when it was illegal. The majority of Thai wildlife exports went to Europe and Japan. Often, species were transhipped to cover their origin, or smuggled together with animals which were not protected.

- The use of wildlife in international trade may conflict with better uses of it in its country of origin. Wildlife may provide food, attract tourists, support local industries. As more Third World countries wish to turn to the rational, sustained exploitation of their wildlife, some control over exports is becoming essential.

* Thailand's wildlife was regulated by the Reservation and Protection Act of 1960 but it was not until it was amended in 1974 to impose new restrictions on the export of animals, that the volume of trade decreased.

* Venezuela banned the export of crocodile hides in 1970.

* Brazil outlawed commercial exploitation of all wildlife in 1967.

* Colombia prohibited trade in skins or live specimens of a number of animals in 1974.

* Kenya prohibited hunting and the commercial exploitation of a number of wildlife products in 1978.

CITES: the first moves

- These problems were discussed at the 7th General Assembly of IUCN (the International Union for Conservation of Nature and Natural Resources) in Warsaw in 1960, when governments were urged to restrict the import of rare animals in harmony with the export laws of the countries of origin.

- In Nairobi in 1963 IUCN considered the international wildlife trade in game trophies, leopard skins, bird of paradise feathers, rhino products, tortoiseshell and orangutans.

- A resolution was passed calling for "an international convention on regulations of export, transit and import of rare or threatened wildlife species or their skins and trophies".

- The first draft of such a convention was drawn up in 1964. The same year the UK Restriction of Import (Animals) Act 1964 came into force, and was regarded as a model for the conservation of animals by controlling imports. However, the act applied only to live animals, as UK customs maintained it was not possible to recognise parts and derivatives of different species. Of the wild cat species, only 44 live animals were imported into the UK under licence in 1973-74. But 87,000 cat skins were also imported - legally and without licences.

- Wildlife trade was again an important subject of discussion at the IUCN General Assembly in Delhi in 1969. IUCN had by this time listed the species which it considered that the new international convention should control. South Africa and the USA had by then both passed legislation to control the import of threatened species. The new African Convention for Conservation of Nature and Natural Resources, signed in Algiers in 1968, had replaced the London Convention of 1933 in regulating the African wildlife trade.

The Washington Convention

- Drafts of what became the Washington Convention were sent to governments by IUCN in 1967, 1969 and 1971. The final draft, based on comments submitted by many governments, by FAO (Food and Agriculture Organisation), by GATT (General Agreement on Tariffs and Trade) and by other organisations, was discussed at a plenipotentiary conference held in March 1973 in Washington DC.

- Eighty states were represented, and a further seven were there as observers. On 3 March 1973, 21 nations signed the convention:

Argentina	Federal Germany	Philippines
Belgium	Guatemala	Socialist Rep. of Vietnam
Brazil	Iran	South Africa
Costa Rica	Italy	Thailand
Cyprus	Luxembourg	United Kingdom
Denmark	Mauritius	United States of America
France	Panama	Venezuela

- The Convention on International Trade in Endangered Species of Wild Fauna and Flora is commonly known as either CITES or the Washington Convention.

- Before the convention came into force 10 states had to ratify it. The first 10 were USA, Nigeria, Switzerland, Tunisia, Sweden, Cyprus, United Arab Emirates, Ecuador, Chile and Uruguay, and the convention came into force on 1 July 1975. By March 1979 there was a membership of 51 states which were parties to CITES (see Figure 1).

- Representatives of the parties meet every two years to review the convention and its implementation. The first meeting was held in Berne, Switzerland, in November 1976, and a special working session was held in Geneva, Switzerland, in October 1977 to discuss technical matters. The second plenipotentiary meeting of the parties was held in San José, Costa Rica, 19-30 March 1979. A special conference, establishing a trust fund to finance CITES was held in Bonn, West Germany, in June 1979.

Figure 1 Contracting and signatory states, and attendance at convention conferences or meetings

Country	Date of signature	Date of ratification or accession	Mar 1973	Nov 1976	Oct 1977	Mar 1979
Argentina	3.3.73		X			+
Australia	21.9.73	29.7.76	X	X	X	X
Bangladesh	7.3.73		X			+
Belgium	3.3.73		X	+		
Bolivia	23.12.74		X			
Botswana		14.11.77	X			X
Brazil	3.3.73	6.8.75	X			X
Canada	2.7.74	10.4.75	X	X	X	X
Chile	16.9.74	14.2.75		X		X
Colombia	4.6.73		X			
Costa Rica	3.3.73	30.6.75	X		X	X
Cyprus	3.3.73	18.10.74	X			
Cambodia	7.12.73		X			
Denmark	3.3.73	26.7.77	X	+	X	X
Ecuador	12.12.74	11.2.75	+	X		X
Egypt	7.6.74	4.1.78	X			X
Finland		10.5.76	X	X	X	X
France	3.3.73	11.5.78	X	+	+	X
Gambia		26.8.77				X
East Germany		9.10.75	X	X		
West Germany	3.3.73	22.3.76	X	X	X	X
Ghana	16.12.74	14.11.75	X	X	X	X
Guatemala	3.3.73					+
Guyana		27.5.77	X			
India	9.7.74	20.7.76	X	X	X	X

Country	Date of signature	Date of ratification or accession	Mar 1973	Nov 1976	Oct 1977	Mar 1979
Indonesia		28.12.78	X	+		X
Iran	3.3.73	3.8.76	X	X	X	X
Ireland	1.11.74					
Israel	5.3.73		X			+
Italy	3.3.73		X		+	
Japan	30.4.73		X			+
Jordan		14.12.78	X			X
Kenya	30.4.73	13.12.78	X			X
Kuwait	9.4.74					
Lesotho	17.7.74					
Luxembourg	3.3.73		X			
Madagascar	4.4.73	20.8.75	X	X	X	X
Malaysia		20.10.77				
Mauritius	3.3.73	28.4.75	X	X		X
Morocco	9.3.73	16.10.75	X	X		X
Nepal		18.6.75			X	X
Netherlands	30.12.74		X	+	+	+
Nicaragua		6.8.77				
Niger	5.3.73	8.9.75	X			X
Nigeria	11.2.74	9.5.74	X	X	X	X
Norway	23.12.74	27.7.76	+	X	X	X
Pakistan		20.4.76	X	X		X
Panama	3.3.73	17.8.78	X			
Papua New Guinea		12.12.75		X		X
Paraguay	30.4.73	15.11.76				
Peru	30.12.74	27.6.75	X	X	X	X
Philippines	3.3.73		X	+	+	+
Poland	8.10.73		X			
Portugal	6.12.74		X			
Monaco		19.4.78				
Senegal		5.8.77	X			X
Seychelles		8.2.77				
Socialist Rep. Vietnam	3.3.73		X			
South Africa	3.3.73	15.7.75	X	X	X	X
Sudan	27.4.73		X	+		
Sweden	3.4.73	20.8.74	X	X	X	X
Switzerland	2.4.73	9.7.74	X	X	X	X
Tanzania	30.4.73		X			+

Country	Date of signature	Date of ratification or accession	Mar 1973	Nov 1976	Oct 1977	Mar 1979
Thailand	3.3.73		X	+		+
Togo	7.3.73	23.10.78	X			X
Tunisia	21.3.73	10.7.74	X			
USSR	29.3.74	9.9.76	X		X	X
United Arab Emirates		20.11.74				
UK	3.3.73	2.8.76	X	X	X	X
USA	3.3.73	14.1.74	X	X	X	X
Uruguay	9.1.74	2.4.75				
Venezuela	3.3.73	24.10.77	X			
Zaire		20.7.76		X		X

X Participant   + Observer

March 1973	Plenipotentiary Conference, Washington
November 1976	First meeting of the Conference of the Parties, Berne, Switzerland
October 1977	Special Working Session, Geneva, Switzerland
March 1979	Second meeting of the Conference of the Parties, San José, Costa Rica

---

The Arabian oryx, now probably extinct in the wild, still breeds in captivity and is now being released back to its natural habitat. It is listed in CITES Appendix I, which means all commercial trade is forbidden. (Drawing: Peter Scott, © Fauna Preservation Society)

CHAPTER 2 WHAT DOES THE WASHINGTON CONVENTION SAY?

- According to its preamble, the signatories to CITES recognise "that wild fauna and flora in their many beautiful and varied forms are an irreplaceable part of the natural systems of the earth".

- They also recognise "that international cooperation is essential for the protection of certain species of wild fauna and flora against over-exploitation through international trade".

- The aim of the convention is to establish worldwide controls over trade in endangered wildlife and wildlife products. The convention itself is deposited with the Swiss government, and has texts in five languages: Chinese, English, French, Russian and Spanish. It consists of 25 articles, outlines of which are given in this chapter. A full text of the convention and its appendices appears at the end of this briefing document.

ARTICLE I defines the terms used in the convention. In particular, it states that the convention covers animals or plants alive or dead, plus "any readily recognisable part or derivative thereof". (This has caused great discussion: enforcement authorities often refuse to recognise parts which scientists consider "readily recognisable". A proposal for a "minimum list" of readily recognisable parts and products was discussed but rejected at the Costa Rica meeting.)

ARTICLE II outlines fundamental principles. Endangered species are listed in three appendices:

* Appendix I lists species threatened with extinction

* Appendix II lists species not yet threatened but which could become endangered if trade is not controlled. Species are also included on Appendix II if they are difficult to distinguish from other species on Appendix I or II. (This is to make it more difficult for illegal trade to take place through misidentification or mislabelling.)

* Appendix III lists species which individual states protect at home and over which they want the cooperation of other states.

ARTICLE III regulates trade in Appendix I species. An export permit from the country of origin and an import permit from the country of importation are required. These permits are issued by national management authorities, provided that they and their removal from its country of origin will not be detrimental to the survival of the species, and that the motive is not for primarily commercial purposes. Live specimens must be properly shipped and housed.

ARTICLE IV regulates trade in Appendix II species. Regulations are less strict than for Appendix I. An export permit from the country of origin is required but not an import permit. Conditions are similar to Appendix I species, but there is no restriction on the specimen's use for commercial purposes. Appendix II helps monitor the trade. Each national scientific authority must record the export permits granted by its country for Appendix II specimens.

Grevy's zebra was placed on CITES Appendix I in 1979, after uncontrolled hunting had greatly reduced its numbers in Kenya. (Drawing: Peter Scott, © Fauna Preservation Society)

ARTICLE V regulates trade in Appendix III species. Imports require a certificate of origin; and if the import is from the state that has included the species on Appendix III, an export permit is required. (Appendix III is not yet used much. It could be useful for generally widespread species which are rare in some countries - for example, the natterjack toad and sand lizard, which although widespread in Europe are now rare in Britain and Scandinavia.)

ARTICLE VI concerns the format of permits and certificates. A separate permit is required for each consignment; an export permit is only valid for six months.

ARTICLE VII relates to exemptions, for which the usual controls on trade need not always apply. Exemptions include:

* a specimen acquired before the convention came into force. (This has led to considerable problems of stockpiling.)

* the re-import of personal property or household effects

* Appendix I species bred in captivity or plants artificially propagated are to be treated as Appendix II species.

* the non-commercial loan and exchange of specimens between scientists and museums etc. (This has led to problems in enforcement)

* specimens which form part of travelling zoos, circuses or exhibitions

ARTICLE VIII describes enforcement, which is the exclusive responsibility of member states. Penalties may include fines, imprisonment, the confiscation of specimens, or their return to the state of export. Rescue centres must be provided for confiscated live specimens. (This has presented considerable problems: very few centres have ever been set up.) Certain ports can be designated for the exit and entry of convention specimens. Records of trade are to be maintained and reported to the CITES secretariat.

ARTICLE IX describes the management authorities and scientific authorities which each state must have. The management authority is responsible for issuing permits, subject to advice from its scientific authority. The scientific authority is expected to notify the CITES secretariat if it believes trade in any species should be limited.

(A management authority is generally a government department. In the UK it is the Department of the Environment; in the US, the Federal Wildlife Permit Office of the Fish and Wildlife Service; in Papua New Guinea, the Conservator of Fauna at the Department of Natural Resources; Nepal has two: the Chief National Park and Wildlife Conservation Office for fauna and the Director General of the Department of Botany for flora; in Ghana it is the Department of Game and Wildlife.)

(Scientific authorities include scientists from institutions, museums, or government departments. The scientific authority in the US has representatives from seven federal agencies. In the UK there are three scientific authorities: the Nature Conservancy Council on overall policy, the Royal Botanic Gardens at Kew for plants, and a group of individual scientists and experts for animals. India also has three scientific authorities: the Botanical Survey of India, the Zoological Survey of India, and the Central Marine Fisheries Research Institute.)

ARTICLE X states that where trade is with a non-CITES country, comparable documents to those required by the convention may be accepted.

ARTICLE XI requires meetings of the parties every two years, to review the working of the convention and amend the appendices. UN agencies and non-member states may attend and speak as observers. Other non-governmental organisations, international or (if approved by their government) national, may do the same unless one third of the parties objects.

ARTICLE XII concerns the secretariat, at present provided by the UN Environment Programme, and sub-contracted by it to IUCN. The secretariat's work is discussed more fully in Chapter 3.

ARTICLE XIII provides for communication between parties and the secretariat when a species is being adversely affected by trade.

ARTICLE XIV states that CITES has no effect on domestic legislation or on other international conventions. States may enforce stricter domestic measures.

ARTICLE XV deals with amendments to Appendices I and II. Any party may propose an amendment for consideration at a meeting of the parties, provided the text has been circulated 150 days in advance. Other states' comments are circulated 30 days in advance. An amendment is adopted by two thirds majority; it comes into force 90 days after the meeting. At the first meeting of the parties (Berne, 1976), 42 species or other groups were added to Appendix I, and 72 to Appendix II. Three were deleted from Appendix I and 6 from Appendix II. The amendments discussed at the 1979 Costa Rica meeting are described in Chapter 6.

Amendments may also be made between meetings, by a postal vote in which half the parties must vote. (So far this method has been little used, but is essential if action is to be taken rapidly as species become threatened. The guanaco was added to Appendix II in this way in August 1978.)

ARTICLE XVI describes procedures for amendments to Appendix III. Any party may submit a list of species for Appendix III. This list is sent as quickly as possible to other parties, and takes effect 90 days later.

ARTICLE XVII provides for the amendment of the convention through an extraordinary meeting of the conference of the parties.

ARTICLE XVIII provides for the resolution of disputes between parties.

ARTICLES XIX, XX, XXI concern signature, ratification and accession. The Washington Convention was open for signature from 3 March 1973 to 31 December 1974. States which signed may ratify the convention at any time. (States which were not original signatories may accede to the convention; they do not need to ratify - they should not be allowed to accede until they have passed legislation to implement CITES.)

ARTICLE XXII states that the convention comes into force in a country 90 days after that country has ratified or acceded.

ARTICLE XXIII states that any party may place a specific reservation on one or more species on any of the three appendices, and on parts and derivatives of Appendix II species. (Australia and France have reservations on some of the marine turtles; Australia, Canada and South Africa have reservations on most whales; and France, West Germany and Switzerland have reservations on some crocodiles on Appendix I, to protect the skin industry.)

ARTICLES XXIV AND XXV refer to the denunciation of the convention (ie withdrawal) by any party, and describe the depository government.

CITES parties

- By March 1979 there were 51 party states - countries which had signed and ratified, or acceded, to the convention (Figure 1). Other states have participated in CITES meetings, but not yet become parties (Figure 2). Some Third World countries do not yet have the necessary scientific advice to accede and administer the convention. Several European countries have still not ratified or acceded, probably because of commercial pressure.

Figure 2 Non-parties attending CITES meetings

Country	Washington March 1973	Berne Nov 1976	Geneva Oct 1977	San José Mar 1979
Afghanistan	X			
Algeria	X			
Austria	X	+		
Burundi	X			
Cameroon	X	+		
Central African Empire	X			
Chad	+			
China, People's Rep. of				+
Czechoslovakia	X	+		
Dahomey	X			
Dominican Republic	X			
El Salvador	X			
Greece	X			
Honduras	X			
Hungary	+	+		
Ivory Coast	+			
Jamaica	+			
Korea (South)	X			+
Lebanon	X			
Liberia				+
Libya	X			
Malawi	X			
Mexico	X		+	+
Mongolia	X			
Rwanda	X			
Sierra Leone	X			
Singapore	X	+		
Spain	X			
Surinam				+
Swaziland	X			
Turkey	X			
Upper Volta	X			
Zambia	X			+

X   participant   +   observer

March 1973   Plenipotentiary Conference, Washington
November 1976   First meeting of the Conference of the Parties, Berne, Switzerland
October 1977   Special Working Session, Geneva, Switzerland
March 1979   Second meeting of the Conference of the Parties, San José, Costa Rica

The black rhinoceros is still poached for its horn, which is used for drinking cups, dagger handles and aphrodisiacs. (Photo: Masood Qureshi/ Bruce Coleman Ltd)

CHAPTER 3   THE SECRETARIAT

- The 1973 meeting in Washington which signed CITES decided to ask the United Nations Environment Programme (UNEP) to take charge of the convention secretariat. UNEP contracted the task to the International Union for Conservation of Nature and Natural Resources (IUCN). The secretariat's offices are at IUCN, in **Gland VD, near** Geneva, Switzerland.

- Initially, the secretariat consisted of only one person plus secretarial back-up, but by 1978 there were three professional officers and two secretaries.

Who pays?

- One of the secretariat's current problems is funding. Although UNEP has financed the secretariat so far, the UNEP Governing Council in 1978 make clear that this could not continue indefinitely. At the March 1979 Costa Rica meeting, the parties agreed to set up a voluntary trust fund, to which they would all contribute, to supplement UNEP finance. Permanent and compulsory contributions, which eventually will replace UNEP funding of the secretariat, were agreed at an extraordinary meeting of the parties in Bonn, West Germany, in June 1979 (see page 80).

- One of the basic functions of the secretariat is to maintain efficient links with party states, and ensure that there is communication among them. Its other main function is to organise meetings of the parties every two years, and meetings of the standing committee. Both these functions require considerable documentation - mostly in the three CITES working languages - English, Spanish and French.

Observers and NGOs

- Unlike many other conventions, CITES allows observers to take an active part at the meetings of the parties, provided they are properly accredited and not more than one third of the parties object.

- NGOs (non-governmental organisations) can take part in most sessions, except those dealing with finance and administration, and have the right to speak. NGOs must be technically qualified in wildlife conservation, and can be either international agencies or national agencies which have been approved by their own governments

- International NGO participants at the meetings of the CITES parties have included the World Health Organisation, UNEP, FAO (Food and Agriculture Organisation of the United Nations), IUCN, the International Society for the Protection of Animals (ISPA) and Conseil International de la Chasse et de la Sauvegarde du Gibier (international council for hunting and preservation of game). National NGOs have included the Royal Society for the Protection of Birds (UK), Friends of the Earth (UK), Society for Animal Protective Legislation (USA), Safari Club International (USA), the Wild Bird Society of Japan, the Pet Trade Association (UK) and the Fur Conservation Association (UK). At the Costa Rica meeting, 55 NGOs were represented, mainly from the USA.

- Some government delegations to CITES, notably that of the USA, have included NGO representatives.

The role of IUCN and the SSC

- IUCN provides the secretariat of the convention on behalf of UNEP. IUCN has provided the administrative and technical back-up at CITES meetings, but has also participated through its Survival Service Commission (SSC).

- The SSC was formed in 1949, to identify endangered or vulnerable wildlife; to identify the causes of threats to species; and to advise on measures to reduce or eliminate such threats. It ensures the accuracy of Red Data Books (which list endangered species).

- The SSC (which is part of IUCN) is represented as an NGO at the meetings of the CITES parties.

- The SSC's chairman is Sir Peter Scott (UK), and its deputy chairman is Dr F.Wayne King (USA). The SSC has a number of specialist groups, whose chairmen are members of the SSC itself. These groups include the Threatened Plants Committee, Elephant Group, Cat Group, Insectivore Group, Turtle Group and Freshwater Fish Group.

- IUCN has close links with the International Council for Bird Preservation (ICBP), which has similar specialist working groups (e.g. on pheasants, birds of prey, bustards). Chairmen of the ICBP working groups also sit on the SSC.

- Each of the SSC specialist groups has its own panel of experts, making the total effective membership of the SSC over a thousand, who serve as a worldwide information network for IUCN and - by extension - for CITES.

Red Data Books

- IUCN's Survival Service Commission prepares and updates Red Data Books, which have been produced so far for mammals, birds, reptiles, amphibians, fish and plants. Since Red Data Books are concerned with endangered and threatened species, their importance to CITES is obvious. The majority of the species listed in CITES Appendix I are also described in the Red Data Books.

TRAFFIC

- The TRAFFIC group (Trade Records Analysis of Flora and Fauna in Commerce) was established in its present form by the SSC in 1976, to monitor international trade in wild animals and plants, with particular reference to CITES.

- Unlike most of the other SSC groups, which are run on an entirely voluntary basis, TRAFFIC has four full-time staff as well as a worldwide network of informants.

The vicuna, which the Incas rounded up and sheared 500 years ago, has been rescued from near-extinction by conservation measures in Peru and neighbouring Andean countries. At present it is on Appendix I, but Peru would like it moved to Appendix II to allow a controlled crop of wool to be exported. (Photo: Sullivan and Rogers/Bruce Coleman Ltd)

CHAPTER 4   HOW IS CITES ENFORCED - AND HOW EVADED?

- It is still too early to assess fully the effectiveness of the Washington Convention. The 1978 annual report of the CITES secretariat states that progress has been made in cooperation between countries. But a large amount of illegal trade still takes place, and that in many instances CITES cannot yet be adequately enforced due to lack of funds and personnel.

- A number of enforcement problems were discussed at the Costa Rica meeting, including standardised forms to document the movement of specimens, identification guides for enforcement officers, standardised taxonomy, standards of shipment for living specimens, and the identification and designation of rescue centres.

- As a result of documentation presented at Costa Rica it became clear that certain countries (among which the UK and West Germany were specifically mentioned) were apparently not enforcing effectively the licensing requirements of CITES.

- Other than the action of individual governments, there is no CITES mechanism to check whether or not the smugglers of wildlife are being apprehended and dealt with effectively. Neither is there any easy way to determine whether or not the national management authorities are functioning effectively and carrying out the tasks required of them under the convention. Twenty six out of the 33 countries party to CITES on 1 January 1977 have submitted complete annual reports for 1977 as required by Article VII.

- Non-enforcement of the convention by member governments is a difficult problem, with no simple solution. The only way CITES can ever hope to be effective is by having a large number of parties, so the expulsion of countries even when they are known to be ineffective would hardly benefit CITES overall.

Forms and permits

- Appendix IV of the convention provides model texts for permits and certificates. But at present the actual format of national documents is far from uniform. This presents considerable problems for customs officers in recognising a genuine permit. As a result, in 1978 official CITES export permits issued by some states were rejected by other states as inadequate or incomplete.

- Conversely, inadequate documents may be accepted. For example, in March 1978, four laggar falcons (Appendix II) were exported from Pakistan to West Germany without official export permits; veterinary certificates had been misinterpreted.

- In Zaire, trade in ivory is officially the sole responsibility of the Ministry of Tourism and Wildlife. In March 1978 it was revealed that the Ministry of Finance was issuing permits to buy and export ivory, which could subsequently be "legally" imported by other countries; this practice apparently continues.

- Surinam and Brazil have strict regulations concerning the export of wildlife. The export of cat skins from Brazil has been banned since 1967 and from Surinam since 1954. Yet the UK, West Germany and other countries apparently imported large quantities of spotted cat skins in 1977 from these countries, which almost certainly lacked the documentation required by the convention.

- During 1978, the CITES secretariat enquired about tortoise imports from Morocco, which had been licensed by the UK CITES management authority. The Moroccan government replied that the export of all fauna from Morocco was banned. Yet under the terms of CITES the UK should have demanded Moroccan export permits when the tortoises were imported to Britain.

Customs and identification

- For the Washington Convention to be effectively enforced, customs officers must be able to identify different species and have a sound knowledge of CITES regulations and documents. A few countries do provide training courses and seminars for their customs officers. Canada, for instance, has prepared a videotaped TV programme, as well as handbooks and demonstration material for all ports of entry and frontier posts. In Switzerland the restricted CITES ports of entry have reference books at hand. Enforcement officers in many countries have access (in theory at least) to experts on particular groups of species.

- Spot checks, however, indicate a very low level of awareness of CITES among customs officers. TRAFFIC has conducted an experiment using a non-endangered cactus - virtually all cacti are subject to control by CITES. The cactus was declared or openly displayed at the customs in the UK, USSR, Switzerland, Germany, Sweden, Denmark, USA, Costa Rica, Panama and Guatemala.

- On no occasion were any questions asked as to the species involved or its origin. In most cases, customs officers appeared to be ignorant of any endangered species legislation, even when the importer himself suggested that the specimen might be controlled.

- In the USA and at Moscow, the plant was either confiscated or the importer was told that it should be confiscated on account of health regulations; in the UK, plant health forms were filled in and signed by the customs officer. In many cases customs officers were under the impression that only commercial imports were controlled and that a single plant could be imported, no matter how rare or endangered.

- A common orchid from France growing in a pot was also imported into the UK by TRAFFIC. Although all orchids are on CITES Appendix II, no action was taken by UK customs.

- Most striking was the import into the UK of a can of whale meat from Japan. The importer actually told the customs officer that this was controlled under the Endangered Species (Import and Export) Act, the UK legislation implementing CITES. Although whale meat imports have been banned longer than most other wildlife products, the customs officer allowed it through.

- Identification of species is a real and difficult problem of enforcement. Identification often involves details of measurements, skin pattern or bones, particularly where subspecies are concerned. It is even more complex where one is dealing with parts and derivatives of similar species, such as crocodile skins, wolf versus coyote skins, or ivory from Asian versus African elephants.

Tourism

- Governments are sometimes inclined to regulate the commercial wildlife trade but not tourism. The tourist trade in wildlife may be substantial. At present there is a worldwide trade in dried turtle shells, which are often bought by tourists.

- The Sudan limits the commercial export of crocodile hides to European tanneries to 60,000 per year. But it allows unlimited killing and stuffing of crocodiles for the tourist trade - it has been estimated that there may be as many as 100,000 in Sudanese souvenir shops at any one time.

- Tourists are usually ignorant of legal controls on wildlife, and often return from Third World countries with souvenirs which are parts and derivatives of CITES-controlled species - for example, stuffed turtles, cat skins, ivory. Airlines and hotels are under pressure from conservationists to play a greater role in publicising CITES, so that the wildlife which attracts the tourists can survive.

Disposal of confiscated specimens

- CITES (Article VIII) states that live animals which are confiscated under the convention may either be returned to their country of origin or be taken to a rescue centre. This presents problems in practice, as considerable expense is often involved in returning specimens, and few countries have yet set up rescue centres.

- For example, two live Asian elephants destined for Japan were illegally imported into Malaysia from Thailand. They were returned to Thailand - at Thailand's expense.

- In 1978 Ethiopia asked CITES if confiscated dead wildlife specimens could be sent to Sweden for auction. This was queried by the secretariat on the grounds that any sale of confiscated Appendix I goods would encourage trade.

- Peru suggested that confiscated specimens could be purchased by parties for use in scientific research, or cultural or educational purposes. The money could be used for a programme strengthening the implementation of the convention. Hong Kong has suggested that the secretariat should act as a central clearing house for confiscated specimens, which could be used for training national enforcement officers.

- The general consensus of the parties at the meeting in Costa Rica appeared to be that, at least for Appendix I species, confiscated specimens should not be traded in any way, except for purely educational, scientific or other purposes directly related to conservation. In other words, they should never enter the market for which they were originally destined.

National reports

- A major problem in the enforcement of CITES is that less than half the nations of the world are yet parties to the convention. Some of these are the key producers and consumers of wildlife.

- Many Third World non-CITES countries (eg Thailand, Tanzania, Zambia, Argentina and Colombia) still lack the resources, finance and expertise to implement the necessary legislation. The consuming countries (eg Japan, Italy, Spain, Belgium and the Netherlands - all of which are not yet parties to CITES) often have powerful commercial lobbies opposing controls.

- As a result, as controls are implemented in one country, commercial activities tend to move to the non-party states.

- Some of the parties have not submitted annual and biennial reports to the secretariat (as required under Article VIII). This means that the secretariat is unable to gauge the volume of trade which is still occurring, and to suggest where changes need to be made. Of the 34 party states in 1977, 26 have so far submitted the reports required. Many of these reports were incomplete; for example, only 11 mentioned trade in plants. According to a rating prepared by IUCN (see Figure 3), only seven out of 26 reports received were substantially complete.

- There is also little correlation in the annual reports on transactions between party states. TRAFFIC has carried out a detailed analysis of the international trade in cats, based on the national reports, in order to evaluate their usefulness and accuracy. The discrepancies may be due in part to different methods of recording and control, but TRAFFIC concluded that many differences were due to inadequate enforcement.

- The incompleteness of many of the reports can be seen when they are compared with the data published in national trade statistics, usually gathered by customs departments. Some of these discrepancies may be due to the fact that customs data may refer to species not controlled by legislation, but this does not explain all of them.

- For example, in their CITES annual report, West Germany listed only 21% of the cat skins which their customs statistics said were imported and exported.

The European Economic Community (EEC)

- The European Economic Community (EEC: Belgium, Denmark, France, West Germany, Ireland, Italy, Luxembourg, Netherlands and the UK) approves of the Washington Convention, considering it an effective means of controlling wildlife trade. But in order for CITES to be effective within the EEC, common steps for implementing it are needed between EEC countries.

- At present, neither Belgium nor Austria are parties to CITES and these countries probably control a large proportion of the world trade in live animals, which includes re-exports to other parts of Europe, North America and Japan.

Figure 3 Rating of 1977 national reports to CITES.
4 = substantially complete; 3 = some data missing;
2 = important data missing; 1 = substantially incomplete;
0 = no report received by 1 March 1979.

	Date received	Rating
Australia	5.4.78	4
Brazil	No report	0
Canada	19.7.78	3
Chile	20.11.78	2
Costa Rica	29.12.78	3
Cyprus	20.2.79	2
Ecuador	18.1.79	1
Finland	1.12.78	3
East Germany	26.12.78	3
West Germany	30.10.78	4
Ghana	No report	0
India	18.10.78	2
Iran	8.10.78	2
Madagascar	25.1.78	4
Mauritius	No report	0
Morocco	No report	0
Nepal	6.11.78	1
Niger	23.10.78	2
Nigeria	No report	0
Norway	9.11.78	3
Pakistan	28.11.78	2
Papua New Guinea	9.5.78	3
Paraguay	No report	0
Peru	18.4.78	3
South Africa	13.9.78	4
Sweden	19.6.78	3
Switzerland	24.7.78	4
Tunisia	20.11.78	2
United Arab Emirates	No report	0
United Kingdom	27.10.78	4
USSR	15.1.79	3
USA	12.12.78	4
Uruguay	18.12.78	1
Zaire	No report	0

- Belgium is today believed to be the major European inlet for CITES species, just as the Netherlands was until recent legislation. These CITES species then find their way into West Germany and other countries. In 1976, for example, a dealer in Holland, "A Man in't Veldt", was publicly advertising the Philippine (monkey-eating) eagle, which is now the Filipino national bird and totally protected.

- The UK also appears to be a major staging post for wildlife going from Third World countries to the USA and to other developed countries. US investigations suggest that a pair of Spix macaws valued at $12,000 were smuggled through Britain in 1978 for a wealthy US collector. While the USA brought 650 prosecutions in 1978 in cases involving illegal wildlife trade, the UK brought less than five; it is unlikely that this had anything to do with the virtue of UK wildlife dealers. Travellers with wildlife products pass very easily through Heathrow Airport, London.

Stockpiling

- Specimens of CITES-controlled species which were acquired before the convention came into force are exempted from certain controls (Article VII), and are issued with a certificate for "pre-convention acquisition".

- This procedure has almost certainly been abused, either by the issue of certificates obtained under false pretences or by the stockpiling of goods in the period before the convention came into force in any country.

- For example, ocelot skins were clearly stockpiled before CITES was implemented in the UK on 1 January 1976. In 1975 up to October ocelot imports from South America were no higher than those for 1974 (about 27,000 skins). Between October and December 1975, 50,000 skins were imported to the UK.

Transit trade and laundering

- A number of abuses of the convention have come about as a result of Article VII which allows transit and transhipment of specimens to be exempted from CITES regulations. Consecutive changes in the destination of illegal shipments are often made to cover up the true country of origin. For example, reptile skins illegally exported via Venezuela are often routed via Panama and cottontop marmosets destined for the UK are routed via Panama and West Germany, to avoid Colombian controls.

- Some parties have already opted for more restrictive national legislation. The CITES management authorities in West Germany and the USA have been empowered by domestic laws to control transit trade as well as exports and imports.

- The UK has no control on transit specimens. In January 1978 a consignment of chimpanzees (Appendix I) was allowed to pass through the UK on its way to Moscow. The Netherlands, although not a party to the convention, has legislation covering endangered species in transit and in December 1978, 10 chimpanzees were confiscated at Amsterdam airport en route to Spain and Mexico from Sierra Leone.

The ocelot, said to have the most attractive fur pattern of all the cats, is the mainstay of the South American fur trade. Exports are banned by many countries, but trade is "laundered" through such ports as Baranquilla (Colombia) and Colon (Panama). (Photo: Harold Schutz/ Bruce Coleman Ltd)

- Transit trade may often be used as a "laundering" device: illegal exports of protected species pass through another country where they receive valid documentation. Important laundry ports for the wildlife trade include Singapore, Baranquilla in Colombia and Colon in Panama (though this may have changed since August 1978, when Panama ratified CITES).

- A further problem with such ports is that they are often free ports, outside customs control. In 1977, large quantities of Appendix II skins were exported from Switzerland to other parties, leaving from the free port zone, Chiasso, which is outside the administrative control of the Swiss management authority.

- Consignments were regularly re-exported from Singapore with legal export documents giving Singapore as the country of origin regardless of the fact that most of Singapore's wildlife was exterminated years ago. Ten years ago, Singapore banned the transhipment of orangutans exported illegally from Indonesia. But in 1975, a Singapore dealer (Mayfield Kennels and Zoo) was still advertising orangutans for sale as well as other protected Indonesian species such as Sumatran rhinos. Singapore now says that it will no longer accept wildlife imports without an official export permit from the country of origin, and as Indonesia has ratified CITES, one of the major problems of the wildlife trade may be on its way to a solution.

- Colombia was a major "launderer" for South American wildlife. Leticia, on the frontier of Colombia with Peru and Brazil in

Amazonia, was given free port status at the end of the 1960s, and huge quantities of illegal hides and skins subsequently passed through. In 1970, 43,417 black caiman hides (caimans are South American crocodiles) were exported from Colombia, where they are fully protected. Leticia also attracted illegal trade from other Amazonian countries, such as Brazil and Venezuela.

- Free port status was removed from Leticia in 1973, and the "Plan Vallejo" instituted. This is an arrangement allowing skins from other countries to be imported temporarily into Colombia tax free in order to process them for re-exporting. In fact, Colombian skins were being smuggled out of Colombia and then being imported as "Panamanian" skins for tanning. In 1975 Colombian lawyer Alberto Donadio brought a lawsuit challenging the validity of the permits granted under the Plan Vallejo and as a result the Colombian government suspended all Plan Vallejo contracts, and an investigation into the smuggling of wildlife and skins out of Colombia was carried out, leading to a final exposé in 1978.

- Leticia is an important centre for cocaine smuggling and it has been suggested that animals such as poisonous snakes have been used as a cover for the much more lucrative drug smuggling trade. Although the animal trade in Leticia was apparently closed down recent reports (late 1978) indicate that it is starting up again.

- Panama has also been affected by the investigation into the Plan Vallejo. Although it is now a party to CITES, Panama was an important transhipment stop for illegal wildlife from Colombia. A passenger flight from Baranquilla airport in Colombia to Panama on 20 February 1978 carried a cargo of the skins of 3,000 caimans (crocodiles), 2,000 boas (large snakes), 1,150 iguanas (large lizards), 100 snakes, 50 parrots, 50 macaws, 50 monkeys, 30 night monkeys. The animals were awaiting re-export at Panama's international airport along with illegal skins destined for Europe and Japan. Arrests have now been made in Panama as a result of the investigation, and the CITES secretariat has asked the Panamanian and Colombian wildlife management authorities to intervene.

- An undesirable side effect of CITES is that the convention has in several countries driven much of the wildlife trade underground.

- Thailand, once heavily involved in the legal wildlife trade, became a centre for illegal trade. In August 1978 a consignment of animals, ostensibly shipped from Laos via Thailand to Belgium, contained three Malayan tapirs, three cats (labelled as "leopard" cats but possibly clouded leopards), 38 white-handed gibbons and 50 stumptail macaques. In fact, much of the consignment probably originated in Thailand: the white-handed gibbons were identified as a race coming from Thailand, while the tapirs could have come from Thailand, Burma or Malaya, but not Laos. Thailand forbids the capture or sale of gibbons or tapirs. The Bangkok Wildlife Company, which was involved in this shipment, is now being investigated by the Thailand Wildlife Conservation Division and IUCN.

- The CITES secretariat has asked the airlines involved in the Thai case to cease shipping illegal wildlife. Since then, Sabena Airlines claim to have refused all carriage of CITES-protected animals between non-party states (Belgium, Thailand and Laos were all non-parties). Swissair will no longer ship live animals other than fish or pets from East Asia to Belgium or Austria. Thai Airways has banned transit consignments of live animals from Laos.

- An important case concerning transit trade and laundering was still under consideration in March 1979. Large stocks of African ivory, mainly from Zaire and Kenya, were being held "in transit" in Belgium without export documents from the country of origin. Most of it is destined for Hong Kong, but because of the recent full implementation of CITES there, the Hong Kong authorities will no longer admit ivory without accompanying export permits. The traders want the Belgian Ministry of Agriculture to issue re-export permits, which would effectively make Belgium a launderer - technically the ivory does not qualify for a re-export permit if it left Zaire or Kenya in contravention of local law - as much of it almost certainly did.

Sanctions

- Contraventions of CITES are still not always treated as serious offences. Where prosecutions have been made, penalties have varied widely, and are often clearly inadequate. Fines are often nowhere near the value of the goods being traded. Recent cases include:

    * In January 1979, the Hong Kong Fur Factory Ltd was fined HK$5,000 (US$1,100) with HK$2,000 (US$440) costs for illegally importing 319 cheetah skins from Ethiopia via a Swiss fur trader; the consignment was valued at HK$200,000 (US$43,900).

    * In January 1979, in West Germany, a fine of DM 4,900 ($2,100) was imposed for the illegal import of a single snow leopard from Pakistan via a zoo in Afghanistan.

The leopard, once distributed throughout Africa and across Asia from Turkey to Korea, has been exterminated in some areas of Africa and depleted almost everywhere. Although forest destruction is one reason, the fur trade is another. (Photo: Norman Myers/Bruce Coleman Ltd)

* In January 1979, a UK shop, the House of Sears, was fined £550 ($1,100) with £50 ($100) costs for offering three leopard skins from Rhodesia for sale priced at £2,000 ($4,000), £1,500 ($3,000) and £750 ($1,500).

* In the USA in 1978 a fine of $87,500 and eight months in prison was imposed for the export of 2,500 American alligator skins valued at $1 million to France via a Japanese firm. The skins were worth approximately $400 each, but the fine was $35 each. The ring leader had already received $140,000 on sales of these skins.

- In some cases, heavy penalties have been imposed. In the US, for example, a year's prison sentence was given in January 1979 for conspiracy to smuggle 12 radiated tortoises from Madagascar.

How recognisable is a product?

- In the UK, Friends of the Earth in September 1978 unsuccessfully prosecuted Eaton's Shell Shop, London, under the 1976 Endangered Species Act for offering for sale 16 polished shells of the hawksbill turtle (Eretmochelys imbricata). Imports of tortoiseshell (as turtle shells are called) into the UK were then controlled only if they were "unworked or simply prepared", ie more or less raw. The fact that the shells had been polished allowed them to be passed as "worked" and therefore unidentifiable specimens, although in fact it made them all the more recognisable as turtle shells. Since then, the UK law has been amended to include polished and worked tortoiseshell and also worked ivory.

- However, even pots of turtle oil, clearly labelled as such, remain uncontrolled on the grounds that the contents are not readily recognisable by UK customs officers.

- This lack of control on worked products still occurs in some countries. Ivory, for example, is exported to non-party states in East Asia in its raw state, where it is carved. It is then legally imported into CITES party states in Europe and elsewhere as the worked product.

CHAPTER 5   THE WILDLIFE TRADE

Overview

- The wildlife trade is greatest in species which supply some form of product, rather than in live animals. Often this is a luxury product, e.g. spotted cat furs, tortoiseshell, ivory, turtle soup, seal and reptile skins. The status associated with such products has meant that high prices are paid and the whole business becomes very profitable.

- For some wildlife products, it has been possible to find some alternative - whale oils can be replaced by synthetic substances which are equally efficient, for example. Imitation furs, reptile skins and tortoiseshell are now of such high quality that to the casual observer it is often difficult to tell the two apart.

- A market will always exist for the genuine article, as the value of it lies in the fact that it _is_ real. This is particularly true for ivory. Substitutes have been found - many kinds of plastic - but they can never replace the genuine material. There have been plenty of _alternatives_ for over half a century, but a _substitute_ would have to incorporate ivory's intrinsic value.

- Trade in live animals is still considerable, though fewer wild-caught animals are probably involved. Figure 4 shows a 1924 advertisement, offering a vast number of exotic animals for sale.

- The wildlife trade has been notorious for its wastage; many more animals are killed or die during capture and when in transit than actually arrive at their final destination. Many more die later, through ignorance by dealers and buyers of their basic requirements or as a result of the fact that they do not adapt to captive conditions. For every young orangutan reaching a zoo (in the past), four adult females had probably been shot and three other young individuals had died in transit.

- Even with the dead products of wildlife there is often enormous wastage. It was estimated that in 1976 two million crocodile hides entered international trade but that in fact half of them were spoiled or of such poor quality that they were unusable.

- With more zoos and their increasing concern with conservation, more species are now being bred in captivity. Museums and zoos still consume surprisingly large numbers of specimens. The US and Canada add about 760,000 specimens annually, a total which includes large numbers of invertebrates. Although this consumption is still far less than that of the biomedical or pet trade, zoos are still consumers rather than producers of wildlife.

- The high prices which can be obtained for rare species has meant that the market remains open for less scrupulous dealers. Many dealers operate under titles suggesting that they are zoological establishments such as Zoopark Corten Rene (Belgium), Siam Zoo (Thailand), National Zoo (India) and the Birmingham Zoological Company Ltd (UK). A recent price list of the Ise-shima Zoological Garden (Japan) offers for sale 244 bird, 192 mammal and 17 reptile species, 40 of which are on Appendix I and 98 on Appendix II.

- Primates in particular are still threatened by the live animal trade, but research is being carried out on alternative laboratory methods such as tissue culture, and primates are increasingly being captive-bred.

- Captive breeding or farming is often unsuccessful. It is an expensive business, and with the more exotic species where little research has been carried out, too little is known about the animal's requirements. Many so-called "farmed" animals have simply been taken from the wild before hatching, or as juveniles, and then reared in captivity. Since there are special exemptions in the CITES convention for captive-bred animals, a number of loopholes have arisen with such specimens. Farming can keep the market open and encourage trade in the wild animals. At the same time, farming can offer a longterm income from a wildlife resource.

Figure 4   Advertisement in "The Aquarist" magazine, published in London in May 1924

PREMIER LIVESTOCK EMPORIUM OF EUROPE

If you require any species of British or Foreign Birds, Parrots or Animals, do not fail to pay us a visit.

Our stock consists of 5,000 small birds, Parrakeets and Parrots. In addition to these, we usually have two or three Chimpanzees and also a fine collection of Monkeys, including the following: Marmozet, Squirrel, Capuchin, Woolly and Rhesus; animals such as Zebras, various Antelopes, Lions, Tigers, Elephants, etc., etc. Amongst the Reptile Stock, there are Lizards, Iguanas, Snakes, etc., from South America, India and Australia.

We have also a very fine collection of Mandarin Ducks, Carolinas, and brilliant plumaged Waterfowl, Scarlet Ibis, Francolins, Egrettes, Sarus and Demoiselle and Crown Cranes.

If you are in the vicinity of Tottenham Court Road, we shall be glad to take you round our showrooms.

Our animals are housed at our Menagerie, 11 High Street, Barnet (at the junction of tram terminus) and all livestock is kept under ideal conditions.

CHAPMAN'S
17 TOTTENHAM COURT ROAD, LONDON, W.1

Phone   Museum 6075.   'Grams: Blackbird, 'Phone, London

- The ultimate aim of any conservation programme is to prevent species becoming endangered. Invertebrate animals and plants have only recently been thought of as needing protection: few are yet listed by CITES. Even when legislation does cover such species it is often not enforced - although the import of cacti into several countries is officially illegal, in practice no control is exercised.

- The sheer volume of the wildlife trade is often surprising. For example, in the USA alone 327 tons of frogs - about nine million individuals - are used in educational and research establishments annually. Again, in July-December 1975, Switzerland imported a total of 62 tons of frogs, mainly for human food (see Figure 5). And in 1976 Indonesia exported 3,160 tons of frog meat to Hong Kong, Singapore, USA, Netherlands and Belgium.

- In 1976, Indonesia exported 270,000 monitor lizard skins, 28,000 crocodile skins, 350,000 snake skins, and 71,000 tortoiseshells, all mainly to Singapore.

Figure 5   Imports of frogs into Switzerland,
July-December 1975, mainly for human food

Country of origin	Weight in tons	Numbers in thousands
Turkey	30	377
Bulgaria	17	214
Hungary	9	112
Yugoslavia	6	70
TOTAL	62	773

The CITES Appendices

- CITES Appendix I had (prior to the March 1979 Costa Rica meeting) 642 entries, Appendix II 262, and Appendix III 78. Many of these are species or sub-species, but entire families or other groups are also listed. (Chapter 6 covers amendments made in Costa Rica.)

- The IUCN Red Data Books (RDB) list about 280 species and sub-species of mammal, of which 156 are gravely endangered and 401 birds of which 130 are endangered. Red Data Books also exist for amphibia, reptiles, fish and plants, although the last is far from complete.

- Many RDB species are on CITES Appendix I or II, but others (for which there is absolutely no likelihood of trade) do not appear. Conversely, some of the species listed on CITES appendices are not in the RDB, usually because although they are not yet rare, they are particularly heavily involved in trade.

- For many Appendix II species, the main threat from trade is the commercial exploitation of products such as furs, skins, food, or specialities such as ivory. They may also be threatened by the pet trade, and for primates biomedical research is the main demand.

- By the time a species qualifies for inclusion in Appendix I, it is usually too rare for large-scale commercial exploitation. So while some Appendix I species, such as the marine turtles and rhinos, are in demand for their products, for most of these the main threat is zoos and private collections.

- Only eight nations have yet made use of CITES Appendix III, which lists species rare in their own country, and for which international help is needed. Uruguay has eight entries, Costa Rica 11, Ghana, 36, Canada 3, Tunisia 6, Botswana 3, Nepal 9, and Mauritius 3.

- Canada listed the walrus and narwhal. Both these arctic species provide ivory, and may be affected by the rise in price of elephant ivory. In fact, it has been suggested that the current level of exploitation of narwhal by the Canadians might be higher than the recruitment of young animals to the population. Other animals on Appendix III include birds, antelopes and a few curiosities such as armadillos and pangolins which are likely to be in demand for zoos.

Marsupials and monotremes

- Many of the species in these groups have very limited distributions, and Australia has stringent export controls on its species. The genus Zaglossus (echidnas) is on Appendix II in order to monitor trade in those species which occur in New Guinea. Several of the marsupials on Appendix I and II are now known to have a larger population size and wider distribution than was previously thought, and so were deleted at Costa Rica.

- These species could become involved in international trade if zoo demand for them increased. Kangaroos and wallabies were once heavily exploited for their fur and leather. In 1913, one and a quarter million kangaroo skins went through the London fur sales. Since a ban on their killing was lifted, kangaroo skins have re-entered trade in large numbers, as kangaroo leather apparently has more strength for its weight than any other leather. Kangaroo meat is used as human and pet food.

Primates: medical research

- Most of the primates (monkeys and apes) on Appendix I are no longer seriously traded in as they have become so rare. For example, only about 1,000 lion-tailed macaques (Macaca silenus) are left in the Western Ghat mountains in India. The tamarins and marmosets listed under this Appendix now have very restricted ranges.

- All the great apes are on Appendix I. Chimpanzees (Pan troglodytes and P. paniscus), although listed as endangered in the IUCN Red Data Book, are still in demand - and scientists will pay enormous sums of money for them. Since 1973, 220-270 have been exported annually from Sierra Leone by two dealers, about 50% going to the USA, 20% to Japan and the rest to Europe and the USSR. Exports from Guinea and Liberia had ceased by the mid-1970s, probably because chimpanzee populations there were so reduced.

- The chimpanzee population in Sierra Leone has recently been estimated at 7,500-12,500, and there are fears that the real figure may be lower. A temporary ban was put on export in 1978, but there has been little attempt to enforce it.

- Chimpanzees have a low breeding potential; even under the best natural conditions a female will only produce three to four offspring in her lifetime. They are also difficult and dangerous to catch, and it appears that the method often used is to slaughter the adults in order to take the young - anything up to four to five individuals may be killed for the export of one young chimpanzee.

- In December 1978, during Sierra Leone's temporary export ban, 10 baby chimpanzees originating from Sierra Leone were confiscated at Amsterdam airport, bound for a circus in Spain and a zoo in Mexico. The US has since said that it will issue no more import licences for chimpanzees, and the chimps have been sent to Gambia for rehabilitation.

- The mountain gorilla (Gorilla g. berengei) provides a striking example of the effect trade can have on a small population. Twenty years ago there were 500 mountain gorillas on the Zaire-Rwanda border. Due primarily to habitat destruction, numbers are down to about 250 today. But there is now a market for gorilla skulls as souvenirs among European tourists and even scientists, and poaching has become a serious problem. At least 16 have been killed for their heads since 1976. In 1978 the dominant male of a troop was killed; this may result in the whole troop of animals dying out as younger animals probably have not attained the maturity necessary to hold the group together.

- All other primates are listed on CITES Appendix II; large numbers are still traded in, mainly for research.

- The macaques are the most important species for biomedical research, notably the rhesus monkey or Indian macaque (Macaca mulatta) from India and south-east Asia; the pig-tailed macaque (M. nemestrina) from south-east Asia, Sumatra and Borneo; and the crab-eating macaque (M. fascicularis) and the stump-tailed macaque (M. arctoides) from south-east Asia.

- The earliest recorded use of primates for scientific research was in 1886 when it was found that rhesus monkeys were reproductively very similar to humans. At the end of the 1940s demand for primates for laboratories was still relatively low but it increased rapidly and reached a peak in the 1950s during the race to develop and produce a polio vaccine.

- Between 1954 and 1960, one and a half million monkeys were used for testing polio vaccines. In the late 1950s, the USA was importing 200,000 rhesus monkeys annually from India alone. The use of primates in vaccine testing has been decreasing in the last few years, as new techniques have been introduced, especially those involving tissue culture.

- Primates make up only 1% of all animals used in research, but they are extremely important. In the early 1970s, 27% of the primates used for scientific research in the USA, UK, France and West Germany went to vaccine preparation and testing; 20% for toxicology studies including cancer; 18% for the study of disease and 11% for physiological studies. Twenty five per cent of the US imports go to the pharmaceutical industry.

- The import of primates for zoos and as pets has decreased considerably over the last few years. Until recently, 50% of the US live primate imports - mainly squirrel monkeys, marmosets and tamarins - went to zoos and the pet trade. In the UK, the primate pet trade has virtually disappeared, largely because of rabies controls. Disease regulations have had a far greater effect on the primate trade than any conservation measures, as the former tend to be more vigorously enforced.

- The most popular research primate is still the rhesus monkey, which in 1949 became the first monkey in space and which became famous for the discovery of the "rhesus factor" in blood. In Denmark and Belgium the vervet (<u>Cercopithecus aethiops</u>) is used most often for research. Japan has its own macaque (<u>M. fuscata</u>), which would be very suitable for a captive breeding management project; Japan, however, still imports rhesus and other monkeys.

- Although only a few species are really important for research, many species have become involved. As one species became rare or was protected another was used instead. An examination of UK imports between 1965 and 1975 showed that as imports of African cercopithecids (Old World monkeys) and cebids (New World monkeys) fell, imports of Asian cercopithecids rose or remained stable. Thus, imports of the vervet or green monkey from Africa fell from 974 in 1968 to 25 in 1975, while imports of the crab-eating macaque rose from 3,574 in 1968 to 4,725 in 1975.

- The world primate trade has declined considerably since the late 1960s; in 1977 the US imported 28,559 primates, 26% of the 1968 imports. Between January and September 1978 the US imported 22,630 primates.

- In 1970, 58% of US primate imports of known origin were from Latin America, 34% from Asia and 7% from Africa. India, Peru and Colombia were the main suppliers but the last two countries banned exports of primates other than for scientific research in 1973.

The mountain gorilla has been reduced to about 250 on the Zaire-Rwanda border. At least 16 have been killed since 1976 for their skulls - which are sold to European tourists. CITES completely bans international commercial trade in gorillas. (Drawing: Peter Scott, © Fauna Preservation Society)

In that year only 23% of the US imports were from Latin America, while Asian imports had increased to 68%. Since then Latin American exports have decreased by a further 71%.

- Prior to the 1973 export ban, Peru had been exporting 35,000 monkeys annually from Iquitos, four fifths of which were squirrel monkeys. The mortality rate between capture and arrival varied from 25 up to 80%. Peru is also said to have killed 7.5 million monkeys for food between 1964 and 1974, compared with the 1.5 million captured for export. Following the ban, exports dropped dramatically; in 1976 Peru officially exported 500 primates, all from managed areas which had been set up as part of a primate conservation programme.

- India used to be the main Asian supplier, in the 1950s exporting around 200,000 rhesus monkeys per year. By 1974 this had dropped to 30,000. In 1975 an annual quota of 20,000 was set, and in April 1978 exports were banned entirely

- The ban on exports from India was imposed as a result of the serious decline in the rhesus monkey population throughout most of its range, largely due to a reduction in its forest habitat. The rhesus monkey population in Uttar Pradesh in northern India was once put at 10-20 million, but in 1961 it was estimated at only one million. Numbers were declining among some groups by as much as 5% per year, and by 1970 this same population had declined to 500,000.

- Sixty per cent of Indian rhesus monkeys now live in towns and villages, where they are regarded as pests, since they raid crops and food stores. Unfortunately, these monkeys are subject to a high incidence of disease and parasite infestation and so tend not to be the ones trapped for export. In other countries, similar problems exist. In Uganda baboons represent a considerable threat to crops and large sums of money have been spent on their control. These animals, which are often healthy, could perhaps be captured and exported thus providing much needed revenue for such developing countries.

- Thailand used to be a main source of macaques and gibbons. Nineteen thousand primates were exported between 1972 and 1975, mainly to the USA and Japan. In 1976, Thailand introduced a total ban on commercial export; a ban had been introduced on gibbon exports 10 years earlier, but illicit trade had continued on a substantial scale until recently when adverse publicity and an increased enforcement effort reduced it.

- As the original major suppliers have introduced export controls, other countries have become increasingly important. The South American trade shifted to Bolivia and Guyana, although Guyana declared a moratorium on the export of all native wild animals in 1976. The Indian ban has put pressure on Bangladesh to increase its exports of rhesus monkeys. Malaysia and Indonesia are becoming increasingly important; 91,000 macaques were exported legally from Indonesia between 1970 and 1975, and numbers have been increasing since then. Current primate imports into Japan and the USA (Figure 6) give some indication of the main suppliers today.

Figure 6   Current primate imports into the USA and Japan
(percentage of total imports in brackets)

	USA		Japan	
Country of origin	1977	1978 Jan-Sept	1977	1978
Bolivia	3,095 (11%)	1,515 (6%)	1,678 (23%)	2,248 (29%)
India	10,139 (36%)	4,882 (22%)	535 (7%)	56 (1%)
Malaysia	3,547 (12%)	4,459 (20%)	1,030 (14%)	1,433 (19%)
Indonesia	-	4,077 (18%)	3,138 (42%)	3,022 (39%)
Other countries	11,778 (41%)	7,697 (34%)	1,019 (14%)	943 (12%)
TOTAL	28,559	22,630	7,400	7,702

- The soaring price of wild-caught primates has been an important factor in encouraging captive breeding. In the mid-1960s, an adolescent wild-caught rhesus monkey cost about £7 ($20) in the UK; by the mid-70s a similar individual cost £50 ($100).

- Unfortunately, captive breeding is expensive. A pair of captive-bred Barbary macaques (Macaca sylvanus) cost about $700 in 1976. At that time it cost twice as much to rear a macaque in a laboratory than it did to import a live specimen. However, cost is not the only factor. Captive-bred animals have known pedigrees and disease histories and so external factors can be better controlled. This has become increasingly important as the quality of imported specimens has decreased. A report in 1979 stated that breeding primates can be cheaper than importing wild-caught individuals for certain purposes.

- At present in the US only 3% of the 70,000 primates required each year are produced by captive breeding. Within five years this figure should rise to 10-20%; the US government is sponsoring commercial breeding programmes.

- At Mount Takasakai National Park in Japan and at Monkey Jungle in Florida, USA, a number of primate species have been bred and reared. Both these projects are costly, however, as the populations are heavily fed.

- The UK has done comparatively little to encourage captive breeding, although one primate breeding centre has been set up by the Ministry of Defence. This expects to produce 20-25 monkeys a year over the next two years, and aims to satisfy a significant proportion of total UK demand by the 1980s.

- In 1967 an attempt was made to "ranch" primates on a large scale in Peru. Some 5,690 squirrel monkeys were released onto an island in the Amazon, and initial reports spoke of a high breeding success. Investigations after a couple of years revealed that there were only a few hundred monkeys left, and that the dealer behind the project had exaggerated its success.

- Peru has since set up successful breeding centres and intensive and semi-intensive management areas for tamarins and squirrel monkeys. By 1982, Peru expects to export 6,500 primates, of which 1,000 will come from breeding centres and the rest from managed areas.

- Most primate species can now be bred in captivity. West Germany is breeding rhesus monkeys, marmosets and tamarins.

Whales and dolphins: the IWC

- A few species of cetaceans (whales and dolphins) are involved in a large volume of trade. Over the years, the species concerned have changed due to successive over-exploitation. Their long life and low reproductive rate make whales easy to over-exploit - and population recovery can take 10-100 years. The female produces only one offspring every 2-3 years, and in some species males may not breed before they are 30 years old.

- The cetaceans are divided into two sub-orders: the toothless baleen whales which have plates of baleen with which they sieve plankton out of the sea; and the toothed whales which feed on fish, cephalopods and warm blooded animals. In the former

---

The humpback whale, the mainstay of the Antarctic whaling industry before World War I, is now entirely protected. It is listed in CITES Appendix I, but population recovery may take decades. (Drawing: Peter Scott, © Fauna Preservation Society)

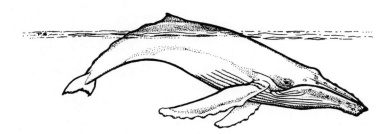

category are the blue whale, the right whale, the grey whale, the humpback whale and other rorquals. The majority of cetaceans are in the second group, and include dolphins, pilot and killer whales, porpoises and the sperm whale.

- The larger species have been most seriously depleted by trade. The blue whale, the right whale, the humpback whale and the bowhead whale are all on CITES Appendix I, but the grey whale is the only protected species which has made any significant recovery. The fin and sei whales are on Appendix II, with part of their populations on Appendix I.

- Until 1979 the only other species listed on Appendix I was the Ganges susu, a river dolphin, but at Costa Rica the proposal to include all cetaceans on Appendix II was accepted. Four species and two genera were also added to Appendix I - these are some of the smaller species such as river dolphins. However, Canada and South Africa have placed reservations.

- The Japanese have had a long tradition of whaling; the European and American whaling industries started seriously in the 17th century. All three regions concentrated on the bowhead, humpback and grey whales, as these moved slowly and so were easier to catch. They were in great demand for their baleen, which was known as whalebone and used for corsetry, riding crops, brooms and other purposes. At its peak price at the end of the 19th century it was worth £2,000 ($3,600) per ton. The sperm whale was not exploited at first; it provides no whalebone and its meat and oil are unpalatable, but by the 18th century it too was in great demand for its oil, used for oil lamps.

- The whaling industry declined considerably at the end of the 19th century, by which time the bowhead and other North Atlantic species had already become rare. Gas and electricity superseded oil, and whalebone was replaced by other materials. In the 20th century the development of new techniques such as explosive harpoons, fast catching boats and the factory whaling ships, plus the demand for oil for margarine, soap and a variety of other modern products, meant that whaling once again became profitable.

- With the depletion of arctic stocks the whaling fleets moved down into the Antarctic. The new techniques meant that larger and faster species could be caught, and the humpback and the blue whale were heavily exploited; 80% of the 1930 whale catch consisted of blue whales. In the 1950s ultrasonic techniques were used for locating whales.

- The species currently exploited on a commercial scale are the sei, the minke, the fin, and Bryde's whale, all of which are baleen whales, and the sperm whale. The sperm and the minke whale now provide most of the world's catch. The sperm whale is important for its oil (which is 80% of its value), which is used as a lubricant in the leather industry.

- Sperm oil prices reached a peak in 1977, when quotas for the sperm whale were lowered. Prices have now dropped to £650 ($1,450) per ton as consumption has dropped and more industries are using alternatives.

- Meat is now the most valuable product from the other species. Eighty five per cent of all baleen meat is consumed by humans (particularly in Japan); in 1976 whale meat sold for $1,000 per ton - a fin whale weighing 50 tonnes would have been worth $20,000 in meat alone. Whale meat is also used for pet food, and to feed mink etc on fur farms.

- Most parts of whales yield profitable products:

    * Ambergris (from the intestine of sperm whales) is used in scent and high quality soaps;

    * Whale blood is used as a fertiliser and in glue;

    * The skin of the toothed and white whales is used as leather for bicycle saddles, handbags, shoes and briefcases;

    * Sperm oil is used for dressing hides, hair oil, shaving cream, lubricating oil, printing ink and detergents;

    * Tendons have been used for tennis rackets and surgical stitches;

    * Whale oil is used for dynamite, medicines, varnishes, linoleums, paint, margarine, lard, shortening, candles and crayons;

    * Sperm whale teeth are carved, and also used for piano keys;

    * Spermaceti, an oily substance in the head of sperm whales, is used for ointment and candles.

- The main agreements concerning the control of whaling are the 1946 convention which established the International Whaling Commission (IWC), and the Permanent Commission of the Conference on the Use and Conservation of the Marine Resources of the South Pacific, which was set up in 1952. The IWC is represented at CITES. (A further convention, the 1931 Convention for the Regulation of Whaling is also still in existence.) Now, 23 nations belong to the IWC (membership has fluctuated continuously) of which the main whaling countries are Japan, USSR, Norway, Iceland, Denmark, Brazil, Korea, Spain, Peru and Chile.

- In 1976, Japan produced 8,400 tonnes of sperm oil, of which 3,365 tonnes were exported. The USSR produced 55,000 tonnes in 1976 - equivalent to 11,000 whales - none of which was exported. Most of Japan's exports of whale oil go to the Netherlands.

- Stocks are classified by the IWC as either "sustained management", "initial management" or "protection", and are exploited according to a quota system. Commercial exploitation of the fin, sei and Bryde's whale is permitted in some areas and of minke whales in most areas of their distribution.

- However, the IWC has no powers of enforcement, and a member nation can dissent from its decisions. In order to retain the membership of Japan and the USSR many damaging compromises have had to be made; in 1972, a 10-year moratorium was called for, but it has never been agreed by the IWC.

- A considerable amount of whaling occurs outside the jurisdiction of the IWC, notably by Somalia, Portugal, China and Taiwan. Whaling is also carried out by "pirate" factory ships; the Sierra Trading Agency is one such organisation, which registers under a non-IWC flag of convenience and takes whatever whales it wants, regulated only by the market.

- In recent years the trade in whale products has declined, mainly because of reduced catches, in turn caused by reduced stocks. UK imports, which come from a variety of countries, dropped from 11,550 tonnes in 1974 to 4,000 tonnes in 1978, due to the rise in prices, uncertainty of supplies and use of substitutes which are now available for all products.

- In 1973, the UK banned the import of all whale meat and baleen whale oil; the UK now bans the import of all whale products except sperm oil, skin and teeth, spermaceti wax and ambergris. The USA banned the import of all whale products in 1971, and New Zealand did so in 1976.

- Many smaller cetaceans, such as dolphins, are sold for exhibition in marine parks and dolphinariums; some of the river dolphins could be threatened by this trade. The narwhal, from the arctic, is hunted for its unique horn which is now worth $1,000 per metre. Canada has listed this species on Appendix III, as there are fears that the current level of exploitation might be higher than the recruitment of young animals to the population.

The international fur trade: spotted cats and others

- The carnivores are the main group of animals exploited by the fur trade, and the excesses of this trade have resulted in many species becoming endangered. A large number are listed on the CITES appendices.

- There are about 36 species of wild cat, of which about half have been or are being exploited by the fur trade. The large scale international cat skin trade started at the end of the 19th century, and by the mid-20th century was a major threat to many species - in particular the tiger, cheetah, snow leopard, clouded leopard and jaguar.

- Cat populations are threatened by other pressures besides the fur trade. As top predators they are very sensitive to changes in prey numbers, and so may be affected both directly and indirectly by any changes in their environment and by habitat destruction. They are also killed by man in self defence, to protect livestock, and for sport.

- Most of the big cats, and a number of smaller cats, are listed on CITES Appendix I; others were added at Costa Rica. All other cats are now on Appendix II.

- The tiger has suffered extensively at the hands of man. There are eight subspecies. The Bali and Caspian tigers are considered to be extinct; there may be about 150 Siberian tigers in the USSR, China and Korea; little is known of the Chinese tiger; the Javan tiger is on the verge of extinction with only about five survivors, and the Sumatran tiger has a population of about 800.

- Only the Indian and Indo-Chinese subspecies are thought capable of survival in the long-term. The Indo-Chinese population may number up to 2,000 and there are sound indications that the Indian tiger is today increasing in number since its dramatic decline. There were an estimated 40,000 tigers in India 50 years ago, but only 1,800 were counted in a 1972 census. One maharajah claimed in 1965 to have shot 1,150 Indian tigers in his lifetime.

- The cheetah (Appendix I) has been badly depleted in Asia and Africa, where it has also had to contend with habitat destruction and agricultural development. Cheetahs are difficult to breed in captivity and so there is also a demand for live animals; at one time it was even fashionable to keep these animals as pets.

- The thick fur of the snow leopard (Appendix I) made it very popular in the fur trade and there now may only be 500 left in the Himalayas and mountains of Asia. Restrictions on international trade have meant that the value of its pelt to the trapper has recently plummeted from $44 to $8, but this species is still being hunted in Nepal by local tribesmen, where it is a traditional demonstration of hunting skill.

- The leopard (Appendix I) is the most widespread of all cats, with a distribution covering Africa and most of southern Asia from Turkey across the USSR to China and Korea. But it has been severely depleted throughout most of its range, and in some regions such as Somalia, Ethiopia and the coastal regions of West Africa it has been exterminated.

- The clouded leopard (Appendix I) has always been uncommon but has become increasingly rare throughout its range from the Himalayas down to Borneo and Malaysia.

- The jaguar (Appendix I) has always been the richest prize for big game hunters in South America, where it is known as the tigre or "tiger"; it measures 1.5 metres (5 feet) from nose to base of tail. An undamaged pelt of a full grown animal was worth $130 in 1976.

- In the 1960s the big cats already showed signs of becoming rare, and so the fur trade turned its attention to the smaller cats such as the ocelot, margay, tiger cat (tigrillo) and Andean cat from South America, the leopard cat from Asia; the serval from Africa, and the lynx and bobcat from Europe and North America. All these except the serval and the Andean cat have one or more subspecies on Appendix I; the Himalayan population of the lynx was moved to Appendix I at Costa Rica.

- The ocelot is supposed to have the most attractive coat pattern of the smaller cats and it is the mainstay of the South American trade. It comes from the forests of South and Central America (extending as far north as Texas) and measures just under one metre (3 feet) from nose to base of tail. The top price for a pelt in 1976 was about $40. Coats, which use 10 ocelot skins each, were selling for as much as DM 74,000 ($40,000) in 1979 in Munich.

- The latest species to be affected by the fur trade are the lynx and bobcat. Prices for a lynx skin on the Canadian market jumped from $40 per skin in 1973 to $150 per skin in 1975. By 1978 they were worth $340, a price similar to leopard and jaguar skins. A good quality lynx coat now costs over $8,000.

- Not surprisingly, the lynx has been eliminated from much of its range in northern USA, although it is still to be found in Canada and Alaska. The bobcat is being similarly affected, and has shown a recent decline in numbers.

- Spotted cats make up less than 1% of the number of skins involved in the fur trade but account for 8.5% of the monetary value. In 1968 the US imported 1,300 cheetah, 9,600 leopard, 13,500 jaguar and 129,000 ocelot skins; Europe probably imported similar numbers. In 1969 the officially-recorded wholesale trade in the US was worth $252,697 for cheetah, $2,105,228 for leopard, $1,672,043 for jaguar and $6,549,537 for ocelot.

- The Brazilian cat trade began to escalate in the 1960s. In 1967 commercial exploitation of all wildlife was outlawed. A period of grace in which stocks could be liquidated was allowed until April 1971, and in 1969 6,389 jaguar and 81,226 ocelot skins were legally exported from Brazil to the USA. Trade has still continued illegally, much of it passing through the Colombian free port of Leticia (on the Amazon) and through Surinam. In the late 1960s about 15,000 jaguars and 80,000 ocelots were being shot in Brazilian Amazonia each year.

- In 1970 Peru extended protection to all wild cats, and in 1973 Colombia prohibited trade in skins or live specimens of jaguars, ocelots and other species.

- In 1971 the International Fur Trade Federation recommended a voluntary ban on trade in snow leopard, clouded leopard, and tiger, and a temporary three-year ban on leopard and cheetah. Unfortunately, this ban had little real effect, especially in France, Italy, Spain, Scandinavia and Japan, and by 1973 the leopard and jaguar as well as the other big cats were clearly endangered.

- Large numbers of skins were still being imported by European countries in 1976 and 1977, as Figure 7 shows. Japan which bought few spotted furs in the 1960s was buying heavily by 1976.

- An analysis of the 1977 CITES annual reports from 16 countries shows that 60% of the skins involved originated from Central and South America (31,700 ocelot, 30,000 margay, 14,600 tigercat and 13,000 Geoffroy's cat) and 27% from North America (26,000 bobcat and 12,500 lynx).

- West German customs statistics, for example, show that over 75% of cat skin imports come from South America, in 1976 mainly from Brazil, and in 1977 mainly from Paraguay. This indicates how flexibly the trade can adjust to new regulations.

Figure 7 European imports of wild cat skins
(data taken from official trade statistics, untanned skins)

		1976	1977
UK	leopard	140	2
	cheetah/jaguar	200	0
	ocelot	9,935	8,408
	other wild cat skins	489,099	42,805
	total skins	499,384	51,215
West Germany	total skins	260,704	300,875
Belgium	total skins	66,833	61,428
France	total skins	22,714	8,670
Italy	total (in kg)	(31,686)	(24,000)

- In 1976 the UK imported 25,878 cat skins from South America (75% from Brazil) and in 1977 14,827.

- Although imports by CITES nations should now be restricted to Appendix II species, a certain number were probably Appendix I animals. such as 442 ocelot skins from Panama and Colombia, 5,436 ocelot skins from Brazil and Paraguay and 17 margay skins from Honduras. In 1977 more than 10,000 skins (including ocelot and margay) which had been killed in Brazil and Colombia were smuggled into Surinam and from there exported to the UK, West Germany, Italy, Spain and the Netherlands.

- In November 1978, 446 ocelot skins and 371 otter skins were confiscated at Lima airport, Peru, destined for a Mr Muller in Frankfurt; the consignment was worth $100,000 and was wrapped in alpaca blankets. In February 1979, 17,538 pelts were seized in Texas valued at $1.1 million. They had been smuggled from Mexico and were destined for sale in Europe. The consignment included 1,500 Mexican bobcats - an Appendix I subspecies.

- 106,700 bobcats were taken in the USA during the 1977-78 trapping season and the US authorised the export of 79,410 skins. According to Canadian customs statistics, 15,345 lynx skins were exported in 1976 and 20,722 in 1977.

- These figures indicate that importing countries must impose more rigorous identification and control measures if CITES is to be effective.

- Different subspecies and even species of the smaller cats are very difficult to tell apart and little is known of their distribution or population sizes. They are often traded under the wrong name, which makes illegal trading in protected species relatively easy. (Ocelot, margay and tiger cat are all often called ocelot or peludo by the trade.)

Seals

- Seals have been hunted by coastal peoples for hundreds of years, for their meat, hides and oil. This regular hunting normally kept populations at steady levels, but when seals were first hunted commercially at the beginning of the 18th century seal hunting rapidly became a large industry.

- Most species are gregarious and come ashore or on to floating ice in large numbers in the breeding season, which makes them easy to kill. In some species such as the harp seal the young are unable to swim during their first month, and so are particularly vulnerable.

- The fur of the fur seals was most highly prized, and these species (particularly the Juan Fernandez and the Guadalupe seal) were eliminated or reduced to very low numbers by the early sealers. The southern fur seals (_Arctocephalus_) are listed on CITES Appendix II (except the Guadalupe fur seal: added to Appendix I at Costa Rica). In 1820-21 all the 250,000 seals of the South Shetland Islands were slaughtered; in 1823 over a million seals were taken from South Georgia and within 50 years the Antarctic fur sealing industry had virtually destroyed itself.

Figure 8   West German 1976-66 imports of untanned cat skins from South America

Country of origin	1976	1977
Brazil	95,411	75,262
Argentina	49,417	13,246
Paraguay	28,839	103,693
Colombia	15,248	4,456
Surinam	2,461	6,358
Bolivia	-	7,580
Other South American countries	12,771	17,716
TOTAL	204,147	228,311

- As with other wildlife product trades, once one species was over-exploited so the trade turned to other species. The elephant seal was extensively hunted for its oil until at the beginning of this century it was almost extinct. The northern elephant seal has increased in number from 20,000 to 50,000 in less than 20 years and at Costa Rica a proposal was accepted to move it from Appendix I to Appendix II.

- Once the southern hemisphere was exhausted, the sealers turned to northern populations. The northern fur seal (Callorhinus ursinus) of the Pribilof Islands was rapidly brought to the verge of extinction. Although regulations existed restricting the annual crop to excess males only (the fur seals and sea lions have a "harem" social organisation - each male has several females and sires many pups) these regulations did not extend to the high seas.

- The first international agreement for the regulation of sealing was the North Pacific Fur Seal Convention of 1911. Many species of seal are now fully protected, although in some cases this protection has come too late. All monk seals (Monachus spp) are on CITES Appendix I but the Caribbean monk seal is probably extinct, and the Mediterranean monk seal numbers less than 500. The grey seal (Halichoerus grypus) has increased in numbers enormously in the UK under protection, and has provoked a considerable debate as to whether and to what extent it should now be culled.

- The walrus is listed by Canada on Appendix III as it is exploited for its tusks which are used as ivory.

- Most of the present major sealing ventures are aware of the dangers of over-exploitation and are managing to avoid it. The northern fur seal on the Pribilof Islands increased in numbers after it was protected to the point where it could again be exploited; the present annual harvest is about 30,000 individuals. About 60,000-80,000 pups and 2,000 adults are taken annually from the Cape fur seal populations off South Africa and Namibia; 11,000 South American fur seals are taken annually off Uruguay.

- The most important species to be harvested at present is the harp seal (Pagophilus groenlandicus). The harp seal fishery reached a peak in the second half of the 19th century, when 800,000-900,000 seals were being taken annually, and were used for leather and oil as well as for fur. Now it is hunted principally for the pelts of the pups or whitecoats.

- The harp seal population was once around 10 million, but by the mid-1960s the world population was estimated at three million, a drop of at least 60%. 282,000 seals were being taken annually off the coasts of Labrador and Newfoundland, the majority of the catch being taken by Canada and Norway and a small proportion (20%) going to the USSR and Greenland and to landsmen from the Canadian coast.

- In 1971 a quota of 245,000 seals per annum was set by the International Commission for North West Atlantic Fisheries, and the Canadian government set up an advisory committee on seals and sealing. The following year the quota was reduced to 150,000 but in 1975 the actual catch increased to 174,000. The quota has again been raised, to 160,000, and there is now disagreement over such basic factors as the true population size and the natural mortality.

The Antarctic fur sealing industry virtually exterminated three species of seals within 50 years in the mid 19th century. In 1820-21 a million fur seals were killed on South Georgia alone. Today, many seal species are listed under CITES. (Photo: Francisco Erize/Bruce Coleman Ltd)

- The hooded seal (<u>Cystophora cristata</u>) is hunted with the harp seal as a secondary source of pelts and its catch had also recently increased, from 7,500 to 15,000 per year, 90% being taken by Norway. Both species have the same close-season, but there are no quotas set for the hooded seal.

- There are fears that over-exploitation of the hooded seal may now be occurring. Although kills by Canada, Norway and the USSR of the harp and hooded seal have been decreasing, the Greenland catch of the the two species has increased by 240% over the last eight years.

- The pelt of the hooded seal is more valuable than that of the harp. Pelts of both seals go for processing either in West Germany or in Norway, and are marketed mostly in West Germany, Norway, France, Denmark and East Germany.

- The **real** value of sealskin has been declining for at least five years, as a result of changing fashion, anti-sealing campaigns, an excess of sealskins on the market, or some combination of these factors. The recent diversification of fur use to novelty items such as coverings for pipes, cigarette lighters, and seal dolls supports the excess idea.

- Seal oil has been increasing in real value, probably because of the decreased availability of fish oils, which have also been increasing in value. At the present rate of increase, oil may once again become the most important product of seals as it was before 1950. It is used principally in food production (eg in margarines) in Canada, Norway and other unidentified European countries.

- The only other product of importance from harp and hooded seals is meat, but it is not involved in international trade. It is used by sealers and by people living in the sealing areas but very few others. In Canada and Norway there are governmental initiatives to improve marketing and extend the sales to other areas and countries. Despite this there was no seal meat cannery in Canada in 1978 - apparently through lack of demand. Most meat is wasted wherever the seals are killed.

- At present there is no sealing in the Antarctic but it is thought that the hair seal populations there could offer good sustainable yields. The crabeater seal (Lobodon carcinophagus) is the most abundant; other species include the leopard seal and Weddell seal. The 1972 Convention for the Conservation of Antarctic Seals will establish guidelines for the regulation of Antarctic offshore sealing should it develop.

- Although seals were not discussed at the CITES meeting in Costa Rica, a number of non-governmental organisations present were pressing for seals and their products to be added to Appendix II so that the trade could be monitored (in particular the harp and hooded seals). There is likely to be much comment on the emotive issue of sealing in the future.

Wolves and bears

- The grey wolf is on CITES Appendix II and is listed as vulnerable by the IUCN Red Data Book. It was originally one of the most widely distributed mammals, but ruthless hunting by man and the decline in its prey species has annihilated it over much of its range. At Costa Rica the grey wolf population of India, Pakistan, Bhutan and Nepal was added to Appendix I.

- In the 1970s, when spotted cat skins became more difficult to obtain, wolf fur became fashionable, especially for men's coats. In the early 1970s the US Department of Defense was fortunately discouraged from using wolf fur for the linings of 277,502 parka hoods; if home supplies had been used, this would have involved killing half the surviving grey wolf population in the USA.

- Of the seven species of bear, the skins of the polar bear, the American black bear and the brown bear (and its subspecies the grizzly) are currently involved in trade.

- The polar bear, also on Appendix II, was until recently badly affected by trade, but the strict protection agreed by all five polar nations (USA, Canada, Denmark (for Greenland), Norway (for Spitzbergen) and USSR) has enabled the populations to recover. During 1976 and 1977, 282 Canadian polar bear hides were sold at an average price of $600 each. Japan is the main market; the potentially large market in the USA is closed as a result of the Marine Mammal Protection Act of 1972 which forbids the import of polar bear skins.

Otters

- The giant otter, the La Plata otter, the Cameroon clawless otter, the southern river otter, the European otter and the southern sea otter, all now on CITES Appendix I, were brought to near-extinction by the fur trade. All other otter species are on Appendix II in order to monitor the trade, as otter skins are difficult to identify to species level.

- Otter fur is rich, dense and lustrous, ranging in colour from dark brown to light fawn; the South American species are the most highly prized. The giant otter, 1.5-2 metres (5-6.5 feet) in length including a 1 metre (3 feet) tail, lives in relict populations in South American rivers. At one time its pelt was worth $1,700 (equivalent to a jaguar) and in 1976 a giant otter coat cost $2,905 in London. Peru exported 2,107 skins in 1946; as a result of over-hunting exports had dropped to 210 in 1966 and there is now little trade.

- In the USA the river otter, <u>Lutra canadensis</u> (Appendix II) is hunted for its pelt. Total annual harvests in the late 1970s were 11,000-15,000. Ninety five per cent of the pelts taken are exported to Europe, and the price of a pelt rose from $25 to $80 between 1977 and 1978. A river otter jacket cost $3,500 in the USA in 1978.

Elephants and ivory: a wildlife investment

- Ivory has been valued as far back in civilisation as the Assyrians and the ancient Greeks. Some of the earliest known paleolithic artifacts are of ivory, and most of the major urban cultures have at one time or another used it. The main source of ivory for carving is elephant tusks, but walrus tusks, narwhal horn, and the teeth of hippopotamus, sperm whale, pigs and many other species have also been used. At one time an important source was the tusks of mammoth fossilised or frozen in ice in Siberia.

- The Asian elephant, listed on CITES Appendix I, now has very reduced populations and is further threatened by habitat destruction and increasing human population in India and south-east Asia. Its numbers were initially reduced by over-hunting for ivory - its close proximity to China and the ivory-carving centres of East Asia meant that it suffered before the African elephant. The supply of Asian elephant ivory is so small now (many bull elephants no longer grow tusks) that it is probably all used locally and little enters international trade.

- The African elephant has a denser ivory which is regarded as being of a higher quality than Asian ivory. The African elephant is on CITES Appendix II, although a few reserves still have large populations. There has been a drastic reduction in numbers over most of its range in the last few years.

- Perhaps because of its durability, ivory has been and still is widely used as a guarantee against inflation. Whenever there is monetary instability, the price of ivory (like gold) increases, often outstripping jewels, paintings or antiques.

- In 1925 the average value of East African ivory was about $6 per kilogram, and in the 1920s Kenya exported less than 20 tonnes each year. Since the Second World War, however, both value and exports have risen. In the 1960s ivory was fetching $7-22/kg and Kenya's ivory exports fluctuated between 15 and 48 tonnes per year.

- In the 1970s very dramatic changes took place. Prices reached $110/kg in the mid-1970s and Kenya's exports rose to 150 tonnes in 1972.

- These high prices resulted in elephant killing reaching an all time peak in 1973-74, which caused a glut on the market. Since then ivory prices have dropped; in 1975 prices were down to $55/kg. However, Japanese imports for 1978 are the highest ever recorded, and high prices remain a strong incentive for both legal and illegal ivory trade to continue.

- In 1976 and 1977, Kenya and Zaire were the main exporters, followed by Uganda, Tanzania, Zambia, Central African Empire, South Africa, Burundi, Sudan, Congo, Somalia, Botswana, Angola and a few other countries. Kenya is a major distribution centre for ivory from many of these sources.

- It has recently been revealed that exports from the Central African Empire increased from 51 tonnes in 1976 to about 200 tonnes in 1978; permits are authorised by Emperor Bokassa himself.

In 1979, CITES was involved in the seizure in West Germany of 141 rhino horns worth $600,000, which had been illegally exported from Kenya. A thousand black rhinos a year are being poached in Kenya alone: this was killed in the Masai Mara reserve. (Photo: James Hancock)

Figure 9   Ivory imports for 1976 and 1977 in tonnes

	1976	1977
Hong Kong	719	476
Japan	310	269
West Germany	71	69
USA	35	15
Spain	34	34
France	17	38
UK	27	18

- The main importing and consuming countries of raw ivory are Hong Kong and Japan, followed by European countries, the USA and probably China.

- Hong Kong and Japan are also centres for the worked ivory trade, as most of the carving is still carried out in the Far East where it is a traditional skill. Over 80% of Hong Kong's worked ivory imports come from China. West Germany is about the only western country to have a developed ivory carving industry.

- Using estimates of 15 kilograms for a pair of elephant tusks in 1976 and 12 kilograms for 1977 (the average weight today is substantially lower) it is calculated that total ivory exports from Africa represented ivory from approximately 70,000 elephants in 1976 and 60,000 in 1977.

- The ivory trade has, not surprisingly, been the cause of dramatic declines in many African elephant populations. Most of the surviving elephants are found in the savannah and rainforests of east and central Africa: Zaire, the Congo, Tanzania, Uganda and Kenya. Tanzania is one of the few countries still with a large population. A survey of the Selous Game Reserve recorded more than 110,000 elephants in 1976-77, but poaching is bad in the north of Tanzania along the Kenyan border.

- In Kenya, elephant populations declined by 50% between 1970 and 1977. It has been one of the countries most severely affected by poaching, and the widespread illicit export of ivory from Kenya in 1975 was shown to involve Margaret Kenyatta, daughter of Kenya's president and mayor of Nairobi. In 1975 it was estimated that Tsavo national park was annually losing through poaching 2,000 elephants out of its 35,000 population.

- The size of the illegal ivory exports can be seen in the discrepancies between the official export figures for Kenya and the official import figures for other countries. In 1974 Kenya recorded exporting 53 tonnes of ivory to Hong Kong, but Hong Kong recorded importing 113 tonnes from Kenya. Similar discrepancies were found in the figures for Kenya, Uganda, Tanzania in 1976.

- Poaching has been increasing in many other African countries where the human population is increasing. Zaire, which has been very conscientious about conservation of its wildlife and specially protects elephants had a large scale illegal trade in 1976. The Ministry of Tourism and Wildlife, which is responsible for the ivory trade, recorded exporting less than one and a half tonnes in 1976, but import statistics of other countries showed that at least 400 tonnes was probably exported via Rwanda, Burundi, the Congo and the Sudan. A large proportion of this was due to the improper issue of export permits by the Zaire Ministry of Finance. Belgium is the main clearing house for ivory from Zaire.

- Ivory, both worked and raw, should now be controlled in the countries which have ratified the CITES convention. The UK initially had no controls over worked ivory on the grounds that it was not "readily recognisable", but in January 1979 UK legislation was amended to include worked ivory. When the UK ratified CITES in 1977, a reservation was deposited which allowed the British colony of Hong Kong to continue to import ivory without any controls. This reservation was withdrawn in 1978, and there are fears that it may drive the East Asian trade underground.

- In December 1978 1,497 elephant tusks worth $100,000 were seized in Hong Kong, having arrived from Zaire without correct documentation.

- In June 1978 the USA added the African elephant to its list of threatened species. The US will in future only allow the import of ivory from states which are party to CITES; those CITES states with significant elephant populations include Zaire, Botswana and South Africa, which altogether account for about 27% of the total African elephant population.

- The US, West Germany, Denmark and Switzerland now refuse to accept carved ivory unless it can be shown that the raw ivory was legally imported.

- Most ivory is finally destined for East Asia, particularly Japan, where there are few import controls. The 1978 figures show that large quantities were still being imported.

- Elephant hide is being used increasingly in the leather trade as techniques have now been developed for processing the whole skin, rather than just the ears which were previously used as they were the only parts thin enough. Hides come from herd culled under government control, but demand is now beginning to exceed supply.

- Since ivory is produced naturally in large quantities each year, there are good reasons for the trade to continue. Ivory could be a valuable resource for many African countries, exploitable on a sustained basis. Since the loss of revenue through ivory poaching is significant, there are strong economic incentives for governments to regulate the trade strictly. One solution could be regulation by a commodity agreement of producing countries, along the lines of OPEC, designed both to maximise long-term revenue and manage elephants as a sustainable resource.

Figure 10 Imports of raw ivory (in kilograms) in 1978 to Hong Kong and Japan (Zaire, South Africa and Botswana alone were parties to CITES throughout 1978).

Country of origin	Hong Kong Jan-Dec	Japan Jan-Dec
Kenya	23,724	47,766
Zaire	21,692	223,858
Uganda	115,881	-
Central African Empire	-	18,416
Tanzania	19,720	10,410
Sudan	29,770	7,392
Zambia	-	6,319
Burundi	6,403	-
Congo	2,574	41,044
South Africa	34,335	389
Cameroons	-	325
Botswana	6,718	2,009
Guinea	-	1,001
Chad	-	1,714
Gabon	-	2,943
Other countries	342,191*	7,342
TOTAL IMPORTS	603,008	370,928

* includes 146 tonnes from Belgium (ie Zaire), and 126 tonnes from France (probably Central African Empire)

Skins, horn, wool, musk

- The wild asses are little involved in international trade but all five subspecies are very rare as a result of over-hunting, disease and competition with domestic livestock. The Mongolian and Indian wild asses are on CITES Appendix I; the other races are on Appendix II.

- Przewalski's wild horse (Appendix I) is probably extinct in the wild now. There have been no reliable sightings since 1968, but large numbers have been bred in captivity.

- Of all the horses, zebras are subject to the greatest pressure from the skin trade. There are three extant species: Burchell's zebra of central and eastern Africa, the commonest though it may become endangered if hunting pressure is not reduced; the mountain zebra of South Africa and Grevy's zebra of East Africa.

- The mountain zebra has two subspecies; the Cape mountain zebra which is on CITES Appendix I and has a population of fewer than 170 individuals limited to a National Park, and Hartmann's zebra (since Costa Rica on Appendix II) which has a limited distribution mainly in Namibia where there may be about 2,000 animals. Hartmann's zebra is subject to heavy poaching and is also in competition with man and his livestock; there were about 50,000-75,000 in the 1950s.

- Grevy's zebra has been over-exploited in Kenya through uncontrolled hunting. It has the most attractive skin of all the zebras: skins on sale in London in 1977 cost $644. The most recent census puts its population in Kenya at 13,000, although in one district numbers dropped from 7,000 in 1977 to 2,500 in 1979, and there is dispute over the census figures. At Costa Rica it was added to Appendix I.

- In 1975 the Kenyan authorities issued 63,000 permits for killing zebras; in 1976 a single hunter was issued with a licence to shoot 200 Grevy's zebras. The 1978 ban on hunting in Kenya might improve the outlook for these zebras.

- All five species of rhinoceroses (three Asian and two African) are on CITES Appendix I, having been extensively hunted for their horn, which is still in considerable demand. Traditionally carved poison-detecting drinking cups were made from rhino horn, and in the Middle East horns are now used for ornate dagger handles - a virility symbol. Despite popular belief, the main demand for rhino horn is probably not for aphrodisiacs in the Far East, which use the waste from carvings.

- In 1975 Kenya officially exported 4,783 kilograms of rhino horn, of which 82% went to Hong Kong and 16% to the Yemen. In 1976 Kenya officially exported 3,339 kilograms, of which 58% went to the Yemen. The 1976 total exports represent some 1,200 rhinos; between 1969 and 1976 11,500 rhino horns were exported from Kenya. Prices have risen dramatically, from $27 per kilogram in 1975 to about $675/kg in 1978.

- In 1978 Japan imported 853 kg of rhino horn, 43% from Kenya and 41% from South Africa. Between January and September 1978, Taiwan imported 802 kg rhino horn (country of origin unknown). The Republic of Korea imported 200 kg rhino horn from Indonesia in 1975, and 50 kg in 1976.

- All three Asian rhinos are now extremely rare, and in Africa both the white and black rhino populations have been drastically reduced. In 1968 there were 11,000 black rhinos in Kenya; by 1977 this had dropped to 1,800. The Africans themselves do not value rhino horn but there is an extensive illegal export trade. Rhinos are usually killed purely for their horn, leading to the serious proposal that wild rhinos should have their horn removed by the game authorities to protect them against poachers.

- The vicuña is currently on CITES Appendix I, and all trade in its wool is banned. This small Andean camel-like animal produces the finest wool in the world (each hair is only 0.0001 centimetres - 0.04 thousandths of an inch - in diameter). Fleeces from a dozen animals are needed to make a single yard of cloth. The vicuña is difficult to domesticate and so it has been extensively hunted throughout its range from south Ecuador via Peru and Bolivia down

Enforcement of CITES is a major problem. Vicuna cloth is still openly sold in London, yet it is illegal to import it into or export it from the UK. (Photo: John A. Burton)

---

into Chile and Argentina over the centuries. (See Chapter 1 for early protective legislation.)

- In the 1950s there were probably between 100,000 and 400,000 vicuñas, but numbers had decreased to about 15,000 by the 1960s. The greatest demand for wool was from the UK and USA; one British manufacturer imported 2-3 tons per year, which is equivalent to about 4,000 animals. The vicuña is now heavily protected and several reserves have been established for it. Its entire population probably numbers 50,000-60,000 animals now.

- In Peru, numbers in the famous Pampa Galeras reserve rose from barely 5,000 in 1968 to over 38,000 in late 1978. But when Peru proposed in 1979 at the Costa Rica CITES meeting to shift vicuña from Pampa Galeras from Appendix I to Appendix II, this was rejected. The decision was reached on the heavy lobbying of the US protectionist NGOs, and was resented by the Latin American states, which saw it as an unjustifiable refusal to allow trade in a sotck which had undoubtedly recovered sufficiently. The vicuña case raises acutely a crucial but largely undebated issue in CITES: is the convention to be used to abolish all trade in wildlife, or to regulate trade so as to maximise it on a sustainable basis?

- The male musk deer secretes the substance known as musk from an anal gland; musk has been used as a fixative in perfumes, soaps and medicine for many centuries. Only 28 grams (less than an ounce) of musk is obtained from a single adult male, and so it commands high prices.

- There are several populations of musk deer in the USSR, Mongolia, China, Korea and in the Himalayas. The Himalayan populations have been seriously affected by illegal trapping and killing, and are on CITES Appendix I. Export of musk from Nepal was made illegal in 1973, but since then musk to the value of over $2 million has been seized - which indicates the extent of the illegal trade.

- Musk deer are now apparently being farmed in the USSR and China; musk can be regularly extracted from an individual deer without having to kill it. Trade in farmed musk should be monitored through the inclusion of the northern musk deer populations on Appendix II.

Birds

- Birds were exploited by man first for food and then for their plumage, which has been used for decorative purposes in many countries over the centuries. With the colonisation in the last century of exotic tropical regions inhabited by colourful birds, a major trade developed in plumage and feathers for decorating hats in Europe and the USA. Demand was enormous and birds were slaughtered wholesale: birds of paradise, egrets, crowned pigeons, kingfishers, tanagers and parrots. Between 1890 and 1929 more than 50,000 tons of plumage were imported into France.

- The import into the UK of bird plumage of most species was prohibited in 1921, and the trade in feathers for millinery has now virtually disappeared. The fly-fishing industry still uses large numbers of feathers; the UK imported 30 kg of skins of Lady Amherst's pheasant from China in 1976 for this industry. Plumes of the grey jungle fowl were used until recently for the manufacture of high quality artificial flies for salmon fishing. The bird itself has received protection in India for a number of years but only recently has the UK banned the import of its plumage; it is now listed on CITES Appendix I.

Figure 11 Up to half a million birds are imported into the UK each year. They come from all parts of the world, but particularly from West Africa and the Indian sub-continent, as the right-hand chart shows.

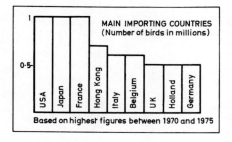
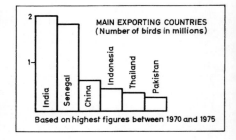

- Birds of paradise (mainly from New Guinea) have always been in demand for their plumage; during the breeding season the males congregate together to display and are easily caught. Many species have very restricted distributions, in some cases limited to only one valley. Most are fully protected in Indonesia and Papua New Guinea and all are listed on Appendix II. However, in 1978 2,000 skins per month were still being exported from Merauke in Indonesia, including at least 500 probably smuggled from Papua New Guinea. Stuffed birds of paradise are a status symbol in Jakarta, where skins sell for $50-75, and stuffed birds sell for $215; Japan is also a prime market. In 1977 Korea was also exporting a wide variety of stuffed birds.

- Ostriches, which provide plumes, skins for leather and eggshells for ornamental purposes have been farmed in Africa for many years.

- The helmeted hornbill is on CITES Appendix I; it was hunted for its bill, the casque of which provided hornbill ivory. This was carved into snuffboxes, etc, and was even more valuable than elephant ivory. It is now only occasionally found in trade.

- The main trade in wild birds is now in live specimens for zoos, private collections, and pets. Aviculture is a very popular hobby. In 1975 the estimated annual international trade involved 7,000,000 birds from more than 100 countries, mainly in Asia, Africa and South America. Most of these are wild-caught; it was estimated that 86% of bird imports into the US in 1972 were wild-caught.

This peregrine falcon was consigned through London Airport from India to West Germany - with a live pigeon as food. Animal welfare organisations collected much of the early data on the wildlife trade. (Photo: Tim Inskipp)

- A study in the early 1970s by the RSPB (Royal Society for the Protection of Birds) in the UK revealed that high mortalities occur in transit. Of the birds arriving at the RSPCA hostel at Heathrow during the years the study took place, an overall average of 4% of birds were dead on arrival; up to 5% may die during the month of quarantine. For some species 50 birds may die for every one that reaches its destination. It has been estimated that at least 80% of the birds at present smuggled out of Australia die before reaching their final destination.

- The UK retail trade is valued at £2 million ($3.4 million), but the actual trappers in the country of export may get little. A study conducted by TRAFFIC in 1977 showed that an Indian trapper may earn one penny (£0.01; 2 US cents) for a bird such as a mannikin; the exporter charges the UK importer five pence (£0.05; 10 cents) and after airline freight charges the UK retailer may have to pay £1 ($2) and the final customer £2 ($4).

- Bird importing into the USA started in the late 19th century. Between 1901 and 1942 14½ million birds were imported, of which the majority were canaries with smaller numbers of gamebirds, parrots and other groups. The development of rapid air transport in the 1930s encouraged the live animal trade, and in the last 20 years the public has demanded a wide variety of species: parrots (in 1974 these constituted 34% of the US total live bird imports), finches, mynahs, toucans and even hummingbirds, sunbirds and other delicate species which are difficult to breed in captivity. This involved the mass removal from the wild of many species.

- The major live bird importers today are Japan, USA, France, West Germany, Belgium, Holland, Italy and the UK. Of India's exports between 1970 and 1976, 49% went to European Community countries, 41% to Japan and 7% to the USA.

- India has been one of the main exporters of birds. Between 1970 and 1976 the annual average export was 1,850,000. Other important Asian exporters have been Indonesia, Thailand, Pakistan, Singapore and China.

- African countries, particularly Senegal and Tanzania, have also been exporting considerable numbers of birds. South American birds are exported in quantity, mainly from Paraguay, Bolivia and other countries lacking adequare export controls.

- Over 20% of the 9,000 world bird species are now involved in trade. Many of these have passed through the RSPCA Animal Hostel at London's Heathrow Airport and their data show that the bulk of the trade is in seed-eating passerines (80%), parrots (10%) and soft-billed passerines (6%). Some species have shown serious declines in their populations in the wild in the last few years, coupled with dramatic increases in price.

- Flamingoes, especially the Chilean and the Caribbean, are imported regularly by zoos as they are difficult to breed in captivity - although Sir Peter Scott's Wildfowl Trust in the UK breeds them in large numbers. Several species are on CITES Appendix II including the Chilean and the Caribbean. In 1978, of 154 establishments in the UK which had birds in captivity, at least 80 kept flamingoes and the total number of birds involved is probably in excess of 2,000.

- Of the 287 species of Falconiformes (birds of prey), 87 are threatened; a large number are on CITES Appendix I and at the Costa Rica meeting, all others were added to Appendix II.

- Birds of prey are often involved in trade, especially for falconry, but until recently few were bred in captivity. The UK imported 1,681 under licence between 1970 and 1976. In 1976 Hong Kong imported 4,273 "eagles" from China and 253 in 1977; controls are now so tight in Hong Kong that this trade has almost dried up.

- Considerable prices may be paid for birds of prey; in the UK in 1979 a buzzard was offered for £85 ($185), a tawny eagle was offered for £275 ($600) in 1978, and the Gyr falcon (which was added to CITES Appendix I at Costa Rica as it is so sought after by Arabs) may sell for up to £20,000 ($45,000).

- CITES Appendix I species include the peregrine falcon, which were often in trade until recently, and the Philippine eagle which is restricted to two islands in the Philippines - the demand for mounted and zoo specimens has reduced it to 30 breeding pairs in the wild and it is unlikely to breed in captivity. (This species was known as the monkey-eating eagle until recently adopted as the national emblem by presidential decree.)

- All owls are now on CITES Appendix II; they are popular in zoos and as pets.

- Pheasants have been exploited by man for many years. There are 40 species, all except one native to Asia, and many are now very rare in the wild although they breed easily in captivity. Appendix I includes the brown-eared pheasant from China and Swinhoe's pheasant from Formosa; the Cheer pheasant was moved from CITES Appendix II to Appendix I in Costa Rica. Controls on trade are necessary as many breeders would like to obtain wild individuals to improve their breeding stock.

- The Houbara bustard and the great Indian bustard were moved from Appendix II to Appendix I at the Costa Rica meeting; they are heavily hunted by Arabs who now go into India as the Middle Eastern populations are so depleted. Their removal to Appendix I should make hunting them in India more difficult.

- The Psittacidae (parrot-like birds) and the passerines (perching and song birds) are the two groups most in demand for zoos, aviaries and household pets.

- Populations of many parrot species have declined as a result of trapping for aviculturists. Many are now seriously threatened, such as the Amazon parrots listed on CITES Appendix I which have very limited distributions. Since the introduction of protective legislation in many countries and the enforcement of CITES, parrots command high prices and a flourishing illegal trade has developed.

- Parrots cost $25 in Mexico but sell for $200 in the USA, and are regularly smuggled over the border. The US found 1,575 smuggled birds between July 1974 and January 1977 and it is thought that this represents only 1% of the total number. However, penalties have been minor compared with the profits that can be made.

- The Mexican yellow-headed parrot (Amazona ochrocephala) is not listed on the CITES appendices and is the bird most commonly found being smuggled out of Mexico. In 1977 a shipment of 350 was seized while being smuggled on a raft across the Rio Grande near El Paso, Texas - they were all destroyed by the US Department of Agriculture under disease control regulations. This species is in great demand as a talker; 1,723 were imported into the USA between 1970 and 1974, and greater numbers have probably been imported since then.

- The Mexican red-crowned parrot (Amazona viridigenalis) and the orange-fronted parakeet (Aratinga canicularis) have been similarly over-exploited, and Mexican parrots are also threatened by habitat destruction.

- The anthill parrots (Psephotus spp.) which nest in termite mounds in Australia include the golden-shouldered parrot and the paradise parrot, both of which are listed on CITES Appendix I. Since Australia imposed strict wildlife export laws, these species have been illegally trapped and smuggled out to America and Europe via South Africa and Belgium. An adult golden-shouldered parrot is now worth $10,000. The orange-bellied parrot (Appendix I) from South Australia and the palm cockatoo (Appendix II) are also involved in this trade.

- Several hundred illegally imported cockatoos worth over $500,000 were stopped by US customs between July 1974 and January 1977. They included 75 rare palm cockatoos which are protected throughout their range in New Guinea and Australia. The price of cockatoos rose from $50-100 in 1975 to about $1,500 in 1977.

- Macaws (large parrots) are still in great demand, and many Latin American countries have tried to restrict their exports; this has little effect as many countries have made no effort and so birds can be smuggled out via them. The hyacinth macaw (Anodorhynchus hyncinthinus) which is not listed in CITES, sells for $5,000-8,000 and a Wagler's macaw (Aracaninde) was advertised by a UK dealer in 1977 for £9,000 ($15,700). Arguably, all parrots should be listed in CITES Appendix II.

- Of the passerines involved in the live bird trade, the hill mynah is one of the most popular, as it is the finest bird mimic known. It is not listed in CITES but has been vastly over-exploited for the European and American markets. The world trade in this species at the beginning of the 1970s probably exceeded 250,000 birds, but India has now banned its export.

- Hill mynahs are usually taken young, often by cutting down trees to get at the nests, which reduces potential sites for this hole-nesting bird. In many countries hill mynahs are now rarely seen outside national parks and the more remote areas. Their UK price rose from £15 ($25) in 1975 to £120 ($200) in 1979. This species is rarely bred in captivity, as birds are usually kept singly in order that they will learn to talk.

- Passerines on the CITES appendices include Rothschild's mynah (which is very rare, confined to one part of Bali, but which was still being offered for sale on a Singapore dealer's list in 1978), and the rock fowls, all on Appendix I; and the brilliant red or orange cock-of-the-rock on Appendix II. The red siskin on Appendix Appendix I is much in demand by canary breeders; it has been crossed with yellow canaries to produce the popular red canary - it sells for about $50 in Venezuela.

Amphibians and reptiles: dying pets and turtle soup

- Several species are still seriously threatened by the pet trade. The metre long giant salamanders (Andrias spp) are on CITES Appendix I having been in considerable demand from zoos and pet keepers; they sold for $100 about 10 years ago. In China and Japan they have been used as food.

- The axolotl from Lake Xochimilco in Mexico is on Appendix II; this neotonous salamander (which retains gills and other larval characteristics throughout life) is severely endangered in the wild but is common as a laboratory animal as it breeds well in captivity.

- The golden frog, on CITES Appendix I, is a very attractive species which, because of its restricted range in Panama, could easily be threatened by the pet trade.

- It has been estimated that in the USA alone, 327 tons of frogs - about 9 million individuals - are used in educational and research establishments annually. These are mainly the leopard frog (Rana pipiens) and the bullfrog (R. catesbiana).

- Switzerland imports vast quantities of frogs, mainly for human food: see Figure 5 (page 30). These are largely pool frogs (R. lessonae) and marsh frogs (R. ridibunda) from Turkey, Bulgaria, Hungary and Yugoslavia: Italy and Greece are also involved in this trade. There are fears that these species may be locally threatened as a result.

- Indonesia exports substantial quantities of frog meat, but the species are apparently not known: 3,160 tonnes were exported in 1976 mainly to Hong Kong, Singapore, USA, Netherlands and Belgium.

- The Tuatara (Sphenodon punctatus) from islands around New Zealand is strictly protected by the New Zealand government. It is famous as a "living fossil", being virtually identical with its Jurassic ancestors. It is of considerable scientific interest and were it not carefully protected, researchers and zoos would almost certainly exterminate it.

- All chameleons are listed in CITES Appendix II, as are Phelsuma geckos, since these are often attractively coloured and popular in the pet trade; they are protected in many of their native haunts.

- The only poisonous lizards - the Gila monster and beaded lizards from the deserts of the southern United States and Mexico - are both listed in order to enforce other protection measures; they are extremely popular zoo exhibits.

- Various terrapins (known as freshwater turtles in the US) and tortoises (land turtles in the US) are listed by CITES.

Turtle soup is still sold in London, and can even be legally imported, because the UK Customs say that it is not a "readily recognisable part or derivative" - which would be subject to CITES control. (Photo: John A. Burton)

- Tortoises have been popular as pets since Greek and Roman times. Mediterranean tortoises have been imported commercially into the UK since 1895. Initially only a few hundred came each year, but they were subsequently imported by the thousand, reaching a peak in 1938 when a quarter of a million were imported, many as hatchlings. Since then over 100,000 have been imported each year; almost as many probably go to West Germany and smaller numbers to other European countries.

- The average life expectancy of an imported tortoise is only a few months; it has been estimated that only 1% of the UK imports survive their first winter.

- Three species are involved. The spur-thighed tortoise (<u>Testudo graeca</u>) makes up most European imports; it is exported mainly from Morocco but increasingly from Turkey. In 1958 it was reported still to be common in Morocco, but a survey in 1969 suggested that it was becoming rarer. Dealers were having to extend their collecting areas further south into hotter, drier areas and the animals from these regions are even less likely to survive European winters.

- Theoretically only tortoises with an undershell of between four and six inches are exported from Morocco. Although this was apparently introduced as a conservation measure, it seems to have been based largely on emotion (ie baby tortoises were attractive but frequently died), based on little or no scientific data.

In fact, it might well be better to exploit the large numbers of surplus baby tortoises than to collect the more mature breeding animals. Tortoises of all sizes are exported from Turkey.

- Animals that are damaged, too large or too small for export from Morocco are used for the souvenir industry, and are turned into banjos, toggles or napkin rings.

- Hermann's tortoise (Testudo hermanni) was formerly exported from Greece, but more recently it has come in fairly large numbers from Yugoslavia and Turkey, probably to make up for the low supply of Moroccan tortoises. Horsfield's tortoise (Testudo horsfieldi) is the third species which is exported in quantity, mainly from southwest USSR, and also from Iran, Afghanistan and Pakistan; it is particularly unsuited to the northern European climate.

- The marginal tortoise (Testudo marginata), Europe's rarest tortoise, is also threatened by the pet trade. Confined to a limited part of Greece, Sicily and a few islands, its restricted range makes it very vulnerable. Although export from Greece is banned, specialist collectors and tourists still collect it.

- UK tortoise imports averaged over 200,000 a year from 1965 to 1975, but in recent years numbers have been falling, possibly because the supply is becoming limited. Based on the UK's figures, an estimated 5-10 million tortoises entered into international trade between 1965 and 1976.

- The Argentine tortoise (Geochelone chilensis) is also collected for the pet trade. Most are exported to Chile and other countries, only 30% arriving live at their final destination. Concern was being expressed in 1978 that the population in Argentina was being severely reduced.

- Sea turtles, all seven species of which are found in tropical and subtropical seas), are exploited for their meat, eggs (important food sources in tropical countries), calipee or cartilage (with turtle meat this is used to make soap), shell (called tortoise-shell) and oil (for soap and cosmetics).

- When the Washington Convention first came into force only the hawksbill and ridley turtles were on CITES Appendix I; the others were on Appendix II. At the first meeting of the parties in 1976 the UK proposed that all sea turtles should be listed on Appendix I. This met with opposition from Australia where the green turtle is relatively abundant, and from West Germany who maintained that this species was not endangered as green turtle product imports into Germany were increasing. As a result of amendments at the 1976 meeting all marine turtles except the flatback and the Australian population of the green turtle (both on CITES Appendix II) are now on Appendix I.

- One argument against the international trade is that turtles can provide a much needed food source in the tropics.

- The Atlantic ridley is almost extinct; it was once found from the Gulf of Mexico north to Massachusetts. The whole population now nests in one place in Mexico, which makes it very vulnerable. In 1947 there were 40,000 nesting turtles, in 1966 there were 1,500 and in 1976 only 256 females came ashore to breed.

- The leatherback, loggerhead and olive ridley turtles have wide ranges, but their numbers are declining rapidly as a result of disturbance at their nesting grounds and exploitation for their meat and eggs.

- The flatback has a limited distribution in Australia; the eggs are collected by aboriginals but this is probably the only species which is not over-exploited and whose population is stable.

- The green turtle has a worldwide distribution but there has been a decline in numbers at all its nesting grounds and at some (eg in Colombia) it is virtually extinct.

- Much of their biology and life history makes turtles vulnerable to exploitation. There is a high mortality at the egg and hatching stage and each female lays between 500 and 1000 eggs in a nesting season, buried in the sand on the beach. Turtles return in huge numbers to nest on the beaches where they were born; this predictability has meant that they are easily exploited. Part of their decline has been due to coastal development on or near their beaches in many parts of the world.

- The hawksbill turtle has been particularly affected by international commerce as its shell provides the best tortoiseshell. It was hunted for its shell from early times until the 1930s when the plastics industry developed and the tortoiseshell market declined. The market returned after the war as people realised that imitation tortoiseshell lacked the beauty of the real product. In 1934 the hawksbill had little monetary value - by 1968 one animal was worth $14. The industry was further helped by tourism in the tropics, and tortoiseshell articles became standard souvenirs.

- The main exporting countries are now Indonesia, Thailand, India and the Philippines (see Figure 12). The total world trade in 1976 probably involved 170,000-240,000 turtles, and in 1977 at least 100,000-140,000 turtles.

- The main consumers and importing countries of raw tortoiseshell are Taiwan, Japan and Hong Kong, followed by other countries in East Asia and Europe. Tortoiseshell is carved primarily in East Asia and is exported in quantity from Indonesia, the Philippines and Taiwan. The main consumers of the worked shell are Japan, France, Italy and West Germany.

- The latest threat to the marine turtles is from the leather trade. Sea turtle leather first appeared in substantial trading in 1965, as crocodile leather became rarer, in particular when alligator hunting was prohibited in Florida. The main centre is Mexico, and the harvest initially concentrated on the Olive ridley turtle until that became endangered. The green turtle from the Grand Cayman Islands, and the hawksbill are now also used, using mainly the flippers.

- Most turtle leather goes to France, Italy, Belgium and Japan. In 1978, Japan imported 94,445 kg of turtle skin, 25% from the Cayman Islands and 43% from Ecuador, and 11,803 kg of turtle leather, 99% from Mexico. A pair of ladies' turtle leather shoes in London cost $108 in 1978.

Figure 12 Estimated total production of raw tortoiseshell, 1977, in kilograms, calculated from statistics of most importing countries

	kg	% of world total
Indonesia	25,992	(27.8)
Thailand	22,190	(23.8)
Philippines	7,193	(7.7)
Malaysia, Fiji, Solomon Is	3,350	(3.6)
Total East Asia and Pacific	58,725	(62.9)
Bangladesh	4,960	(5.3)
Kenya	2,753	(2.9)
India	2,424	(2.6)
Tanzania	1,836	(2.0)
Burma	1,100	(1.2)
Mozambique, Seychelles, Maldives etc	1,252	(1.3)
Total Indian Ocean	14,325	(15.3)
Cuba	3,984	(4.3)
Cayman Is	3,875	(4.1)
Haiti	1,173	(1.3)
Jamaica	1,136	(1.2)
Dominican Republic	1,000	(1.1)
Puerto Rico, Dominica etc	1,785	(1.9)
Total Caribbean	12,953	(13.9)
Panama	4,450	(4.8)
Nicaragua	2,573	(2.7)
Belize, Costa Rica	371	(0.4)
Total Central America	7,394	(7.9)
ESTIMATED WORLD TOTAL	93,397	(100)

Turtle eggs taken from the wild are sometimes reared in captivity ("farmed"), before the turtles are killed for food and leather. Some conservationists support turtle farming as a means of reducing pressure on wild populations; others consider that the presence of farmed turtle products in the market encourages the illegal taking of wild turtles. This stuffed green turtle was photographed on a boat in Thailand. (Photo: John A. Burton)

- The first prohibitive legislation for marine turtles was passed in 1620 by the Bermuda Assembly which prohibited the killing of young turtles. Since then, little action has been taken, except in Australia. In the 1930s, a closed season for turtle hunting was introduced in Australia and now six species are protected along 3,250 miles of Queensland coast and along 1,250 miles of the Great Barrier Reef. This legislation was, for once, enacted before the populations had become damaged.

- The migratory habits of turtles mean that intergovernmental agreements are needed to protect them from excessive exploitation. In 1970, Panama, Nicaragua and Costa Rica agreed to stop exploitation for three years while methods were found for exploiting the turtles on a sustainable yield basis. The situation is still serious, however, although increasing action is being taken.

- Most recently the Convention on Conservation in the South Pacific (1976) has agreed to take action on endangered species by setting up national parks.

- Turtle exploitation has often been justified on the grounds that turtles are, and can be, farmed. (Turtle soup sold in England is often labelled "farmed turtle".) Turtle farming was first tried in 1907 in Curacao but failed. The only large "commercial" farm is Cayman Turtle Farm Limited (previously Mariculture) in the Grand Cayman Islands, Caribbean. The eggs are taken from the wild and originally the yearlings were released back into the sea on the assumption that yearlings would have a better change of survival and that these could then be harvested at three years old. After the first year, however, the hatchlings were no longer released. After 10 years the farm is only having marginal success at breeding their own turtles and eggs are still taken from the wild. This cannot be termed real farming and the presence of turtle products obtained in this way on the market may encourage the illegal taking of turtles from the wild.

Reptiles: towards crocodile farms

- The reptile skin trade is directly responsible for the fact that many species of crocodiles, alligators and caimans are now endangered. As in other wildlife trades, one species after another was exploited as others became rare or were protected and so so no longer useful commercially.

- The reptile skin trade was at its peak in the 1950s and early 1960s, when 5-10 million hides of crocodiles and alligators were being traded every year. By the late 1960s crocodiles were becoming so rare, and the caimans from South America had been protected in so many countries, that dealers were going out of business.

- In addition, finished reptile leather products require skilled handwork by individual craftsmen, which was becoming very expensive. This, with wildlife conservation publicity, may have contributed to the decrease in the use of reptile skins by the leather trade.

- This decline did not last long, however. The trade moved to monitor lizards, pythons, tegus, iguanas, wart snakes, cobras and a wide variety of smaller snakes. Skins began to be processed in Hong Kong and Singapore and the Far East where labour is cheaper.

- At present, in spite of the Washington Convention, the reptile skin trade is thriving and consumer demand is still very high. At the 1978 Spanish leather trade fair, reptile leather was much in evidence including crocodile, lizard, snake (especially whip-snake) and turtle.

- Five alligators, 10 crocodiles and four monitor lizards are listed on CITES Appendix I, and all other species in these group are on Appendix II. Some iguanas are on Appendix II, and a number of snakes are also listed.

- The Mississippi or American alligator was badly affected by the skin trade, but in the 1960s protective legislation was introduced throughout its range. By 1970 its total numbers were estimated at about 500,000 with rapidly expanding populations in Florida and Louisiana. In the IUCN Red Data Book it has been listed as out of danger; commercial trapping is once more permitted to keep the population level down.

- A strong argument against allowing it to enter international trade again, is that it could be used as a cover by dealers in other species. However, at Costa Rica the US proposal to remove it from Appendix I to Appendix II was accepted.

- The situation is not so good for other species. The Chinese alligator (CITES Appendix I) from the Far East is quite probably extinct, having been exterminated for its meat and leather.

- The caimans from South America, as well as being hunted for their skins, are taken in large numbers for the pet trade, or are stuffed for souvenirs. The black caiman (Appendix I) was one of the most important in the skin trade and is now almost extinct over most of its range. The Rio Apaporis and the broad-nosed caiman were both important for their skins; both are on Appendix I and the latter, from Argentina, is almost extinct.

- Of the caimans on CITES Appendix II, the spectacled caiman was one of the most important in the skin trade but its numbers are declining or have disappeared throughout most of its range. The brown and the Yacare caimans are also important in the trade. These latter three are all still in trade, in spite of being listed as endangered in the IUCN Red Data Book.

- The Nile crocodile (Appendix I) has a range which extends throughout Africa. It has the best and most valuable skin of the African crocodiles, and not surprisingly has been badly affested by hunting. The slender-snouted and the dwarf crocodiles (from west and central Africa), were both extensively used in trade, and are now endangered and on CITES Appendix I.

- The Siamese crocodile (Appendix I) from Thailand is known in the trade as "Singapore large grain" and gives a good yield for handbags and fancy leathers. There are now fewer than 200 left in the wild but it is being farmed near Bangkok.

- Of the other crocodiles, the saltwater (C. porosus), which has a wide range in the Indo-Pacific, is one of the most valuable. It is listed as vulnerable in the IUCN Red Data Book, but is still traded in as "Singapore small grain". The New Guinea freshwater crocodile from Papua New Guinea and East Indonesia is also very valuable in trade but is listed as vulnerable in the Red Data Book.

- These species are now being managed in Papua New Guinea, caught from the wild when young and reared in village "farms". Since this is thought to cause no pressure on wild populations, Papua New Guinea was allowed to trade C. porosus internationally as an Appendix II species by the CITES Costa Rica meeting; all other populations of this species were added to Appendix I - until now C. porosus was heavily commercialised in Indonesia.

- France claims to have evidence that the Nile crocodile, the slender snouted crocodile, the broad nosed caiman and the black caiman are not endangered, and has therefore placed a "reservation" on them, allowing French imports despite the CITES listing. France also maintains that the Nile crocodile is only endangered in Madagascar and so should be on Appendix III for Madagascar. It will take some time to finally prove the eligibility of these species for Appendix I, and in the meantime French tanners will continue to import these species in large numbers.

France, Germany and Switzerland have also placed reservations on
C. porosus, which could mean that they will import animals from
Indonesia, which now bans the export under CITES.

- The monitors are the most important lizards in the skin trade.
The species listed on Appendix I have all been heavily involved,
except for the Komodo dragon which is now very rare but could be
threatened by the zoo trade. The Nile monitor on Appendix II is
the most valuable on account of its fine grain.

- Snakes are threatened not only by the skin trade but also by
habitat destruction and the fact that many are killed by man, in
self-defence and accidentally by cars. The Indian python on
CITES Appendix I has been exported in large numbers from India
for the skin trade; and its meat is a speciality with the
Chinese. Other snakes used in the trade include the anaconda
from South America (one of the best-wearing snake leathers) and
the reticulated python from south-east Asia.

- Asia and South America are the main producers of reptile skins.
In 1976, India exported almost 3½ million reptile skins (over
3 million snakes) and Indonesia exported 649,000 skins (54% snake
and 42% "iguana"). In the same year, Thailand exported 64 tons
of reptile skins (30% crocodile and 30% snake) and Singapore
exported 187 tons (60% crocodile).

- Ninety five per cent of Japan's lizard skin imports for
1978 came from Asia, including 56 tons from Bangladesh, 22 tons
from Singapore, 19 tons from Indonesia and 14 tons from Pakistan.
The 1977 CITES annual reports showed that monitor lizards were the
most important species involved. Malaysia and the Philippines
also export considerable numbers.

- India used to be an important source of snakeskin. The industry
boomed in the 1950s, when one tannery in Madras was processing
5-10,000 skins per day. Several tribal groups became full time
snake-catchers and suppliers, and one side effect of the overkill
of snakes was that rat infestation reached a peak. Bernhard
Grzimek, then director of Frankfurt zoo, estimated that 12 million
snakeskins were involved in trade each year - enough skins for a
snake belt round the world. In 1976 exports of raw snakeskins
were banned in India.

- In 1978 Japan imported 15 tons of snake skins, 41% from
Indonesia, 30% from the Philippines, and 20% from Thailand.
China probably imports large quantities of snakeskins as well;
in 1976 Hong Kong imported 490,853 snakes from China and in 1977,
191,540.

- South America exports mainly caimans, iguana, tegu and false
monitor: Tegu (Tupinambis spp.) is one of the most popular lizard
skins. In 1977 the US imported 29,292 pairs of shoes, 8,000
other leather goods and 308,714 skins of tegu. Paraguay,
Colombia and Panama are particularly important exporting countries.

- In 1978 Japan imported 103 tons of alligator and crocodile
skins, 78 tons of which came from Latin America and were therefore
mainly caimans; 54% were from Paraguay and 20% from Colombia.

That year Japan imported 12 tons of alligator and crocodile leather, 6 tons of which was from Paraguay. The USA imported 280,572 reptile skins between January and September 1978, 64% of which came from Latin America; 69,000 skins from Panama and 109,000 skins from Paraguay.

- The African countries export mainly crocodile and Nile monitor. Kenya exported 3,000 crocodile skins in 1976. In 1978 Japan imported 734 kg of alligator and crocodile skins from Nigeria and 170 kg from South Africa; in 1977 the UK imported 400 kg reptile skins from Sudan and 296 kg from Nigeria.

- The main importers of reptile skins are France, Japan, Italy and West Germany, followed by the USA, the UK and Singapore. France currently uses around 500,000 crocodilian hides per year, and West Germany uses approximately 350,000 crocodilian hides per annum, mainly from South America. Italy is an important processor of crocodile skins, with 90% of their production exported. Spain tans large numbers of reptile skins, much of their supply coming from Malaya.

- Japan has four reptile tanneries, the largest of which, Inoue and Company Limited, processes about 650 million skins per annum.

- The UK imported 16 tons of undressed reptile leather in 1977 (valued at $596,000) and 2½ tons of dressed reptile leather valued at $296,000. In 1978, a Singapore crocodile handbag in London cost $1,062; even the raw hide of a crocodile with a 12-14 inch belly width now costs $166.

- Up until 1978 when supplies became too difficult, Mappin and Webb in London were selling about 10,000 lizard bags a year; 6-12 lizards are required to make one bag.

- The high prices of reptile skins has led to a significant illegal trade, particularly in South America. Until 1973, much of the trade passed through the free port of Leticia in Colombia. With the introduction of the Plan Vallejo in Colombia further loopholes were found for illegal trade, as described on page 25.

- In Bolivia many more skins left illegally in 1977 than the decreed quota of 150,000 and as a result the whole future of Bolivian crocodilians is endangered. In June 1978, 25,000 crocodiel skins were confiscated in Rio de Janeiro, but the illegal trade is hard to combat and is encouraged by the high overseas demand. Skins are carried packed between other skins or in bales of cotton and smuggled from Brazil into Paraguay or Bolivia. In one month in 1977 more than 30,000 caiman skins entered Surinam from Brazil.

- Several countries have introduced stringent controls on exports and imports. India has included monitors, snakes of all varieties and several CITES Appendix II species on Part A of its Export (Control) Order 1977, which means that exports of the raw skins are not normally allowed. The reptile leather trade in several importing countries has been annoyed by this; they say that there are large stocks of skins in India which now cannot be used.

- A German expert on the trade, K.P.H. Fuchs, has suggested that all crocodile-producing countries should require hides to be tanned before permitting their export. Since there are fewer tanners than there are trappers and collectors, it would be easier to regulate their illegal activities, and any raw skins exported would be evidence of illegality. Some South American countries do in fact require skins to be tanned before export and India also exports mainly tanned skins; the main problem is that the international leather industry is still willing to purchase illegal, untanned hides.

- The US, Switzerland, West Germany and the UK all now have import controls on reptile skins. Italy has few import controls, saying that CITES would be difficult to enforce since it lists the scientific names of species, and trade names may not correspond with particular scientific species.

- Control has helped create a demand for imitation reptile leather, especially in the USA where fake crocodile handbags sell at up to $330; there is also great activity in producing more convincing simulated reptile leather, particularly in Italy.

- Legislation and decreased supplies is changing the trade. Smaller species are being used, and used more economically. At one time only the flanks and belly of the caiman were used, but now the whole skin is used.

- Crocodile farming, like turtle farming, has been rarely successful, but it does have potential, and the increase in value of skins has made farming economic. It can be expensive; on a Florida farm, 2,500 alligators were eating 3,000 lbs (1,400 kg) of meat and fish a week, but in areas where there are supplies of cheap offal and unmarketable fish, this is not a problem. The main argument against farming is that it sustains a market for skins, which encourages the continuation of poaching and illegal trade. In many cases the word farming is used to describe rearing in captivity, as many of the species needed by the trade have not yet been bred in captivity.

- Samut Prakan crocodile farm near Bangkok began in 1950 with 20 wild crocodiles. In 1960 it hatched 150 and in 1975 3,500 crocodiles. In 1978 the farm had 23,000 animals, mainly the Siamese crocodile (of which there are only about 200 left in the wild) and the saltwater crocodile. The farm has 60% hatching success and 5,000 animals are slaughtered annually for their skin. The farm may, however, have helped cause the decline of the Siamese crocodile in the wild; wild skins can be exported under cover of farmed ones, and the farm still takes juveniles from the wild.

- In Papua-New Guinea crocodile skin exports are closely controlled as part of a government plan to harvest crocodiles as a village industry. There are already over 200 farms, some with up to 1,000 crocodiles. About 30,000 people traditionally depend on crocodiles for their only cash income and since crocodile meat is an important part of their diet it is in their interests to manage the supply. Currently, 30,000-50,000 skins are being exported annually.

- The species involved are <u>Crocodylus porosus</u> and <u>C. novaeguinae novaeguinae</u>; a minimum size limit of 20 inch belly width for legally exportable skins has been set. Strictly speaking, Papua New Guinea does not "farm" crocodiles but captive-rears wild-caught juveniles. At present the programme is not satisfactory for <u>C. porosus</u> as hunting for wild adult hides is still occurring. However, if the populations can stand the present pressure, they may develop into the best-managed crocodilian stocks of the Pacific area, if not of the whole world.

- Farming attempts have also been made in Rhodesia and South Africa where crocodile populations have seriously declined - in South Africa 40,000 crocodiles were shot in one region in seven years, and the crocodile is virtually extinct. However, in 1978 these farms were not running as commercial enterprises.

- If markets can be found for other products from crocodiles (as has been done in Thailand and other parts of the Far East) farming could be very profitable. Reptiles put on weight and grow much more rapidly in proportion to their food intake than most domestic animals.

Fish

- The few fish that have appeared on the CITES Appendices so far are mainly those threatened by pollution, such as the sturgeons. The aquarium fish trade has yet to be fully investigated, but it is known that large numbers of species which are difficult to breed in captivity are taken from the wild in South America. However, much of the aquarium trade depends on captive-bred fish.

Molluscs - shells for tourists

- The two families of molluscs heavily represented on the Appendices (the <u>Unionidae</u> on Appendix I and the <u>Hydrobiidae</u> on Appendix II) are not yet in trade but are endangered by pollution and could be threatened by collecting for museums etc.

- Molluscs have been exploited by man for food ever since the Stone Age, and shell jewellery has certainly been worn for hundreds of years. At the end of the last century shell collecting became fashionable in the same way that butterfly collecting had done. However, these collectors had little effect on wild populations and it is only since the 1960s, with the boom in tourism in tropical countries, that shell collecting became a serious commercial activity and seriously threatened mollusc populations.

- As with butterflies, it is the more expensive and exotic species which are in greatest demand: conches, tritons, cowries, helmet shells and other colourful species of the coral reefs in the Caribbean and Indo-Pacific. They are collected live from reefs, often indiscriminately, which leads to great wastage and frequent damage to the coral. The countries with the most desirable species include the Philippines, Papua New Guinea, Hawaii, East Africa and the Seychelles.

The trade in sea shells has become highly commercialised in recent years, and in some areas the larger specimens and species have become very rare. Some shells sell for up to $250, but CITES has not yet listed many molluscs. This shop window was in Mombasa, Kenya. (Photo: Sue Wells)

- The green tree snail <u>Papustyla pulcherrima</u> (Appendix II) of Manus Island, New Guinea, is one of the few non-marine species popular with collectors; it is also used for jewellery on account of its pretty green colour.

- <u>Mytilus chorus</u>, a Chilean mollusc, the only other mollusc on the appendices involved in trade, was added to Appendix II at the Costa Rica meeting.

- The Hawaiian shell trade has greatly increased over the last five years with the increase in tourists from the USA and Japan. Native species have been depleted on the reefs and this has caused inflated prices; in 1977 a Hawaiian tiger shell cost $75. In 1976 Exotic Shells, a firm in Hawaii, imported and re-exported shells all over the world, selling primarily to non-scientists, and buying huge quantities and selling by the 100 pound (45 kg) batch. They were also selling 250 lb (114 kg) giant clam shells (<u>Tridacna gigas</u>) from the Philippines, which were used in the USA as wash-basins.

- In Papua New Guinea the shell trade is government controlled, and highly organised. Coastal villages have one man responsible for the collection of the shells, and the quality is strictly regulated. Collecting areas are changed regularly, and only specimens of a certain age and size are allowed to be taken.

- Japan, the USA and Europe are the main consumers, as is the case with most wildlife products. Tropical Sea Shells is a new business recently set up in England, selling at first three tons of shells a week. Prices ranged from 3 cents to $232, the average price being about $3, for shells from the Philippines, East Africa and the Seychelles. By the end of 1978 Philippine traders were sending poorer quality shells, which suggests that stocks were being depleted.

- In 1978 Eaton's shell shop in London was offering giant clams at £45-300 ($80-480) per pair, and tritons at up to £25 ($40) each pair.

- Few studies have been made on the shell trade and its effect on mollusc populations, but one in Kenya in December 1978 is probably illustrative of the situation in other tropical countries.

- Legislation passed in Kenya in 1968 made it an offence to collect shells without an official permit. Since 1975 collectors have been restricted to taking a maximum of 5 kilograms (11 pounds) of shells at one time.

- In Mombasa in December 1978 two shops and 10 street stalls were selling shells; in Malindi there were eight street stalls, and hawkers were seen on the beaches and at hotels. There was little evidence of any major international trade, although according to the official trade statistics Kenya exported nearly 90 tonnes of coral and shells in 1977.

- All the stalls and shops tend to sell the same selection of shells, mainly the large, colourful, shiny ones attractive to tourists, such as cowries, spider conches, helmet shells and tritons.

- Much of the Kenyan coast was formerly rich in these species, but the main collecting areas are now restricted to the northern and southern extremities of the coast: Kiunga, Lamu and Shimoni. A few years ago lorry and plane loads of shells were to be seen leaving these areas but such large scale collection has apparently ceased. Three marine parks have been established, where it is forbidden to collect shells; although poaching does occur, there is general agreement that shell numbers are higher within the parks than without.

- As yet no species has become extinct as a result of the shell trade. But the popular species are becoming more difficult to find, particularly the helmet shells and tritons, and large specimens of any species are rare. Equally serious is the damage to the reefs caused by collectors, both tourists and Africans; stones are overturned and the animals living underneath are left exposed to the sun.

Butterflies: the Taiwan connection

- Until the beginning of the 1970s, conservationists had been concerned primarily with threatened birds and mammals. Then public attention was drawn to the scale of the butterfly industry in the Far East. Proposals for protective legislation for butterflies led to a wider awareness that all types of wildlife were becoming endangered through man's activities.

- Butterfly collecting has been popular for over one and a half centuries, reaching a peak around the end of the 19th and the beginning of the 20th centuries. It has only recently become a profitable commercial activity. Early collectors probably collected a wide number of species and had little effect on their populations. As butterflies became fashionable, the more beautiful ones became increasingly popular and were used for decorative purposes. Some used in trade now may come from old collections and some are being bred in captivity, but the main trade is in freshly collected material.

- The birdwing butterflies (mainly Ornithoptera) from SE Asia and Australasia nave been particularly affected and they are now listed on Appendix II. These belong to the Swallowtail family - the males are the most beautiful and they reach large sizes. Queen Alexandra's birdwing (O. alexandrae) is the largest, and has a wingspan of 20 cm (8 inches). This species and the paradise birdwing (O. paradisea) are among the most prized, and also have the most restricted ranges, in isolated localities in Papua New Guinea and nearby islands. The rarer species reach $200-1,200 a pair or even more, and supply cannot meet the demand.

- Taiwan is probably the most important exporter of butterflies. The Japanese introduced butterfly collecting when Taiwan was part of the Japanese Empire. The butterfly industry has flourished since 1945 when the island was returned to the Chinese, and now about 20,000 people including 10,000 collectors make their living from the industry. About 20 million butterflies are caught per year, attracted to urine-soaked sand, and sold to more than 30 factories, each one processing up to 2,000 butterflies per day. 1969 exports from Taiwan were valued at $30 million.

- Papua New Guinea used to be an important source of birdwing butterflies until all export was controlled. Export of birdwings is also controlled in Australia and the Solomon Islands and several South American countries have banned the export of the rarer species; Brazil exported over 50 million butterflies annually in the mid-1960s.

- The main market is Japan, where in 1964 there were 40,000 members of entomological societies. Europe and the USA are also important importers. In 1976, a UK dealer had $300,000 worth of Papua New Guinea butterflies on display for sale. Although some countries have export bans, no countries seem to control the importation of dried insect specimens (apart from the few species listed on CITES).

- With the increase in demand and the enforcement of protective legislation, prices started to increase. In 1972 the UK Daily Telegraph urged readers to buy rare butterflies as a hedge against inflation: in 1969 over $1,875 was paid for a single birdwing. These prices encouraged the development of illegal trade, and protected species were regularly on sale in the UK. Saruman, one of the main UK butterfly dealers, listed a large number of rare or protected species in their catalogue. In Japan, the Insect Educational Centre was selling birdwings for up to £45 ($75) each; another Japanese dealer offered the rare Rothschild's Birdwing for $850 a pair.

- Two European dealers were fined and deported from Papua New Guinea in the early 1970s but in about 1975 there were still three Japanese and three Europeans operating there. The CITES 1976 annual report for Papua New Guinea states that illegal trade (often involving sending butterflies by mail) still occurs with Australia, USA, Japan, UK, West Germany and France; recent prosecutions have resulted in a diminution of the trade.

- In 1978, Raymond Straatmann was deported from Papua New Guinea for his part in large-scale smuggling of Queen Alexandra's birdwing and other protected species, often through "respected scientists". He was receiving as much as $800 for a single specimen.

- It is difficult to determine the effects of such trade on wild populations. Although no proper research has been done, entomologists visiting East Asia have remarked on the apparent decline in butterfly numbers. The destruction of rainforest is in many cases having more effect than trade. Butterflies are mainly found in the hardwood forests, which are being cleared fastest.

- In Taiwan no moves have apparently been made to protect or manage the butterflies, but the Chinese Information Service said in 1975 that more than a dozen farms have been set up to preserve and cultivate rare species. It is not known what success these have had. Butterfly farms in other countries are often simply just centres trading in imported species, whilst breeding a few common species. Papua New Guinea, however, has established a butterfly farming project very successfully, and captive-bred specimens in good condition may well eliminate the demand for inferior wild specimens.

Sponges: a case for action?

- Four hundred different "types" of sponge are recognised in commerce. They all belong to the genera Spongia and Hippospongia, which each contain about six species and/or subspecies: the taxonomy of this group of sponges has not yet been satisfactorily worked out.

- The highest quality sponges come from the Mediterranean, where the honeycomb is the commonest and is the one usually sold as a bath sponge. Fine solids and fine cups are rarer and more expensive.

- In the West Indies, the wool (or sheepswool) sponge is the most valuable, and is similar in texture to the honeycomb but not as soft. The velvet sponge was exterminated in a blight which struck the West Indies sponge beds in 1938, and is now thought to be extinct.

- Commercial sponges are found in the Mediterranean east of Tunis, and in the Caribbean off Florida, Cuba, the Bahamas and to a lesser extent off Honduras and Mexico. A few poor quality sponges are found in the Red Sea, the Arab/Persian Gulf and in Malaya, the Philippines and north Australia.

- No artificial sponges have yet been made which combine the softness, absorptiveness, compressibility, resilience, and lightness of the natural product. Natural sponges are still used in the pottery industry, and they are in considerable demand as bath sponges.

- Although sponges have been in use since Greek and Roman times, the sponge fishing industry started on a commercial basis at the beginning of the 19th century on the Greek islands of Kalymnos and Symi. The discovery of the North African sponge beds, and improvements in methods and diving dress, meant that the industry was booming by the beginning of this century. Diving is the principal method used in the Mediterranean.

- Sponge fishing became commercialised in the West Indies in the 1840s, the main method used there being hooking. Cuba and the Bahamas were major exporters but a combination of storms, a blight which struck the sponge beds in 1938 and severe overfishing meant that the beds virtually closed down. As early as 1900 it was realised that the beds could be easily over-exploited if no controls were implemented. In spite of introducing minimum size limits and closed seasons, the beds continued to be depleted and now almost nothing is produced.

- The Bahamas exports, which reached 700 tonnes at their peak at the beginning of this century, are now down to an annual average of 25-50 tonnes. The Mediterranean has been less ruthlessly exploited and is now the major producer but between 1964 and 1976 Greek exports fell from 111 to 70 tonnes, and Tunisian exports from 90 to 60 tonnes.

- The importer who deals with 70% of the UK sponge trade has said that sponges are becoming increasingly difficult to find. They have virtually disappeared from shallow waters, and now have to be obtained by diving. The Greeks are the only nation with diving expertise, but now have to fish off the coasts of other countries as their own coast has been so overfished. Legislation is apparently not enforced and it seems that the trade itself would be interested in seeing fishing controlled.

Plants: cacti and succulents

- Far less attention is paid to endangered plants than to endangered animals, even though one in ten of the estimated 250,000 different plant species are said to be rare or threatened. These tend to be concentrated in the most vulnerable and species-rich habitats: islands, tropical moist forests, arid lands, Mediterranean ecosystems, wetlands and coastal sites.

- A large number of plants are likely to go extinct before their possible value to society is known. Every year, at a rate rather slower than that of plant extinctions but still very regularly, new and important uses for obscure and little known plants are found. In the last 10 years the jojoba (Simmondsia chinensis) from the south west of the USA has become important for its oils, which are similar to those obtained from the threatened sperm whale, and it is now being planted experimentally as a crop.

- Many endangered plants may be potential crops - at present the bulk of man's agriculture is based on less than 30 species. The Yeheb nut (Cordeauxia edulis), a bush from the Ethiopia-Somalia border, is listed in the Red Data Book, but has great potential as a crop plant in the Sahel, since its nuts have a relatively high protein content, it can grow in very arid regions, and it requires little in the way of cultivation.

- The main threats come from agriculture, over-grazing, and felling for fuel and timber; industrialisation and pollution have also contributed. More recently, a number of plants are being threatened by horticulture. The increased prosperity of the developed countries has meant that many plant species are now exploited for non-essential uses and hobbies.

- A number of species are now listed on CITES Appendix I, including several aloes, orchids and cycads. Cattleya skinneri, the white nun orchid, is the national flower of Costa Rica.

- CITES Appendix II includes whole groups and families of plants: all cacti, a number of tree fern and cycad families, the succulent euphorbias, aloes and all orchids. At Costa Rica, a number of Australian families were added. Many of the plants on the appendices have very restricted distributions in the wild, although they may not be involved in trade at present or may be artificially propagated.

- The cacti and succulents are an important part of the horticultural trade, although the majority of plants are propagated in nurseries. However, a report in 1978 exposed the problem of cactus "rustling" in Arizona. For a few years drought-stricken home developers have been turning to cactus plants for landscaping their gardens. The plants became so popular that demand exceeded supply and a black market developed. Rustlers stole cacti, Joshua trees and yuccas, some of which may have taken a century or more to grow.

- In 1977, 60,000 cacti were harvested legally in Arizona and an additional 20,000 were taken by poachers. This over-exploitation is beginning to cause severe soil damage and erosion.

- Arizona introduced tough protection laws to deter poachers; a special permit is required to harvest any of the state's desert plants and violations can bring up to $1,000 in fines and a year in jail. But the law is difficult to enforce. Cactus rustling is reported to have spread to other states; California introduced protective legislation in 1977.

- There is also a large market for cacti (Appendix II) and succulents (some families on Appendix II) in Europe, and the TRAFFIC group has recently carried out a survey of the trade in the UK. Propagated cacti make up the bulk of the trade, and probably only 15-20% of the imports are collected from the wild. Total imports of cacti into the UK increased considerably from 29,015 in 1976 to 44,890 in 1977. Most of the UK imports come from other European countries (Holland, Malta and Belgium) or from the USA and Israel, and are probably propagated in nurseries. Holland, Belgium and West Germany are the main centres for the cactus trade, and their nurseries depend on habitat-collected (wild-collected) imports for a large proportion of their trade.

- Prices of habitat-collected plants go up to £12 ($20) for a 15 centimetre (6 inch) diameter Aloe polyphylla and £25 ($40) for a multiheaded clump of Ariocarpus.

- The Cactaceae are restricted in the wild to the Americas, apart from a handful of species in Africa and Madagascar. The main countries of origin are Chile, Bolivia, Argentina, Peru, Paraguay,

Uruguay, Mexico and the USA. Import statistics do not distinguish between habitat-collected plants and propagated plants, but plants from countries such as Bolivia and Chile are likely to be habitat-collected as the horticultural industry there is poorly developed.

- Mexico is the home of many species highly prized by collectors. A Stuttgart travel firm (Ehlers-Reisen) lays on "cactus study tours" to Mexico; the trip in 1978 reportedly resulted in the uprooting of an entire population of a very rare cactus (a species of Mammillaria). Fifteen suitcases were apparently bought in Mexico to transport the plunder back to Germany. The 1979 tour was fully booked, but the CITES secretariat had asked Mexico to take action to ensure specimens are not exported illegally. In fact, 3,600 species of cacti were brought back; all were confiscated at Frankfurt airport and a court case is pending.

- The International Organisation for Succulent Plant Study has discouraged the purchase of habitat-collected plants, and cactus societies often mark down such specimens in competitive exhibitions, and refuse to accept advertisements for them in their journals. But in the US at the First Eastern Cactus and Succulent Conference in October 1978 the "Best of the Show" award went to a very rare Ariocarpus known only from one location in northern Mexico.

- Import licences for the Old World succulents increased in the UK in 1977. Licences were granted for 1,003 Pachypodium species, 3,082 Euphorbia, 505 Anacampseros and 52,336 Aloe - more than all the cacti licences together. Pachypodium plants are raised in Europe increasingly, due to the ready availability of seed probably from South Africa and Madagascar.

- Madagascar exported 15,500 kilograms of Pachypodium seed to West Germany in 1977. Presumably this was habitat-collected seed, and there are some fears that although trade in plants may be controlled, large scale trade in seed could, in a few cases, be a threat to the normal regeneration cycle of the species. Some plant conservationists feel that more succulents should be listed on CITES in order to monitor the size of the trade in these species.

- Of the other species listed on the CITES appendices, orchids (Appendix II) are traded in extensively. The 1976 UK CITES report showed that 17,000 orchids of 160 genera were licensed for import from Madagascar, the Philippines, Guatemala, Colombia, Brazil, Mexico and Thailand. Many of these may have been propagated, but some species were certainly habitat-collected and protected in their country of origin.

- Wild orchids are being traded in ever increasing quantities from Irian Jaya to Jakarta (within Indonesia) and elsewhere. Five thousand rupees ($11) may be paid for good specimens.

- Ginseng is believed to combat fatigue and relieve symptoms of stress. American ginseng is harvested extensively mainly for foreign markets especially in the Far East although ginseng is grown in Asia. In past years wild ginseng had consistently sold for higher prices than the cultivated plant. Since 1978 only 17 states have been allowed to export wild ginseng.

- A large number of other plants could be listed by CITES.
One example is the Venus fly-trap, whose survival is threatened in
its one native area - the coastal plains of South and North
Carolina. Although it is possible to propagate these insect-eating
plants, whole communities are collected and sold by mail order.
Most subsequently die, as they are very difficult to look after.

- The Animal and Plant Health Inspection Service (APHIS) in the
USA estimated that in 1977, 38 million plants subject to CITES
were imported into the USA, virtually none of them with permits.
In 1978 enforcement was stepped up, however. Previous imports had
included rare cycads from South Africa, allegedly stolen from
botanical gardens.

CHAPTER 6   THE SECOND CITES CONFERENCE: COSTA RICA, MARCH 1979

- The second conference of the CITES parties (the 1977 Geneva
meeting was only a technical session, with no plenary powers)
was held 19-30 March 1979 in San José, Costa Rica. Delegates
representing 39 CITES parties attended, and a further 15 states
were present as observers (see Figures 1 and 2 for names).
Additionally, the European Community, three UN agencies, and
55 NGOs (non-governmental organisations) were represented.
At least 35 of these NGOs were US or US-based.

- The next CITES conference was provisionally fixed for 1981,
in New Delhi, India.

- Two documents which provoked considerable discussion, were
Doc 2.6 Annex 2 (which revealed that substantial numbers of cat
skins were being exported illegally from Surinam, Peru and Brazil,
without export permits, and being imported to the UK and West
Germany) and Doc 2.5 Annex 8 (which described the wildlife traffic
between Bangkok and Brussels, and the correspondence which the
CITES secretariat has had concerning it).

- The UK, Switzerland and West Germany proposed that CITES should
adopt a "minimum list" of parts and derivatives of listed species,
on the grounds that there was wide disagreement among member states
on just what parts and derivatives were "readily recognisable".
This proposal was opposed by other countries, plus many of the
conservationist NGOs, on the grounds that it would soon become a
"maximum list". The minimum list was rejected by a narrow majority.

- Australia suggested that the increase in trade in non-CITES
wildlife was a negative result of the convention. Other countries -
notably Botswana and Brazil - disagreed strongly. They wanted to
encourage trade in commoner species, as the rational exploitation of
a natural resource. India, on the other hand, anticipated that
before long it might ban all wildlife exports, of any species.
This discussion relates to a fundamental difference in conception
of the convention. Is CITES (as its preamble suggests) a means of
gradually reducing all trade in wildlife, because this commerce
is undesirable? Or is it, on the contrary, a means of regulating
trade in a natural renewable resource, with a view to maximising
its utilisation in the long run, as many wildlife-rich Third World
nations believe? The vicuña debate (see below) also reflected this
dilemma.

The American buffalo or bison, which once roamed the Great Plains in tens of millions, was exterminated by the white man in the 19th century. CITES is increasingly concerned to encourage the wise exploitation of wildlife, rather than to give it complete protection. (Drawing: Peter Scott, © Fauna Preservation Society)

- There was some discussion of the desirability of <u>trading in hunting trophies</u> of Appendix I species. It was agreed that culling of Appendix I species might sometimes be necessary for effective management, and that it was not incompatible with CITES for tourists and sportsmen to pay to shoot the surplus animals, or to sell the trophies. Botswana and Zambia argued this case particularly strongly.

- CITES agreed to establish a <u>standing committee</u> to advise the secretariat between conferences. The countries elected consisted of Zaire (representing Africa), Nepal (Asia), the UK (Europe), Brazil (South and Central America), the USA (North America) Australia (Oceania), Switzerland (the depositary government) and Costa Rica (the present host government).

- The conference called on party states to produce regular, prompt and detailed <u>reports</u> on the wildlife trade in their countries. It also called for greater uniformity of <u>permits and certificates</u> issued under CITES.

- The conference decided that <u>confiscated specimens</u> of Appendix I species should never be allowed to re-enter the commercial trade, but that physical destruction of them should be considered a last resort. The CITES secretariat was asked to establish a clearing house for the international exchange of confiscated specimens - for educational use, or to help customs officials in identification.

- It was agreed by the parties that UNEP should be asked to provide funds for the continuation of the work in preparing an international

loose-leaf identification manual for CITES countries. The US
tabled some sample sheets of an <u>identification manual</u> relating
to crocodiles, and Switzerland demonstrated its own different
system.

- A proposal to abandon the use of <u>subspecies</u> in the CITES
appendices was modified; only valid and readily recognisable
subspecies should now be included. Alternatively, a species
could be included for only one or two countries within its
geographical range.

Finance

- Since its inception, the CITES secretariat has been supplied
and financed by the UN Environment Programme. UNEP has sub-
contracted this task to IUCN (International Union for Conservation
of Nature and Natural Resources), but has continued to provide the
money.

- The UNEP Governing Council decided in 1978 that the CITES party
states ought themselves to finance CITES, and determined to phase
out UNEP funding completely by the end of 1983. The 1979 CITES
conference had therefore to make some moves towards this, but was
restricted in what it could do because any compulsory contributions
from parties would require an amendment to the convention. CITES
decided to call an extraordinary meeting of the parties to do this.

- In the meantime, the Costa Rica conference approved a two-year
1980-81 budget of $984,800. Of this, $350,000 will come from
UNEP, and the balance will be contributed voluntarily by the
CITES parties, according to the recognised UN scale. This will
involve the US paying 25% ($246,000) and Cyprus, Guyana, Papua
New Guinea, Senegal, Paraguay and 12 other small states paying
$98.48 each.

- In Bonn in June 1979 the parties to CITES held a special meeting
to amend the convention and empower the CITES conference to "adopt
financial provisions". These provisions take the form of a
<u>CITES Trust Fund</u> to which all parties will contribute. This
amendment was carried by a 22-1 majority, and will now be
submitted for national approval by each of the parties.

Changes to the appendices

- Although a large number of proposals was submitted, a high
proportion of them was withdrawn, usually because insufficient
data was presented by the proposers.

- Australia proposed the deletion of several <u>marsupials</u>, and the
addition of a few. These proposals were all based on recent
information which shed light on the true status of the species
concerned.

- The only change in the listing of <u>primates</u> was the downgrading
of <u>Cebuella pygmaea</u> (pygmy marmoset) from Appendix I to Appendix II,
since it is known to have recovered in numbers.

- A number of Australian mice were removed from the appendices as they have been found to be commoner than originally thought.

- Some of the most drastic changes were with the whales and dolphins. Most of the river dolphins were added to Appendix I, and all whales, dolphins and porpoises not in Appendix I were added to Appendix II.

- The conference asked all CITES parties not to import any whales or whale products which came from any species or stock protected from commercial whaling by the International Whaling Commission; and encouraged all CITES parties to adhere to the International Whaling Convention.

- Three species of South American fox (two of which are heavily traded in) were added to Appendix II, and a fur seal was transferred from Appendix I to Appendix II. Proposals to remove or downgrade cat species were either withdrawn or defeated.

- Grevy's zebra was added to Appendix I, and Hartmann's zebra was added to Appendix II. The lechwe was dropped from Appendix I to Appendix II, as there is evidence that there are now substantial numbers.

- Chile proposed to downgrade all vicuña from Appendix I to Appendix II; this was heavily defeated, because in most countries vicuña are still rare. Peru proposed to shift only the Pampa Galeras populations of vicuña to Appendix II - a much more acceptable proposal, since this reserve has been carefully managed for over 10 years, and numbers have increased from under 5,000 to almost 40,000. Brazil called the Pampa Galeras vicuña "the best managed natural resource in Latin America", and Peru now wants to crop the vicuña and sell the wool. However, the conservation groups lobbied and spoke strongly in favour of its retention on Appendix I, and the proposal was rejected. It was argued that the La Paz treaty on the conservation of the vicuña (Peru, Chile, Bolivia, Ecuador and Argentina) was being renegotiated in September 1979, and that any CITES changes should wait until after that date. In fact, Peru had stated that she did not intend to start trading in vicuña wool until 1980 at the earliest.

- A certain sense of having been manoeuvred by the US-based protectionist NGOs (the US government had supported Peru) led 21 delegations to call for the issue to be reopened. A vote was taken, which was two short of the two thirds majority needed to reconsider it. Peru may now take the issue to a postal ballot within CITES.

- The two most significant changes in the birds were the addition of all birds of prey, both nocturnal and diurnal (except New World vultures) to Appendix II. This will enable close monitoring of owls, hawks, eagles and other species, which are often highly vulnerable to threats from trade, especially falconry.

- The major reptile changes were the addition of yet two more crocodiles to Appendix I - the American crocodile (Crocodylus acutus) (US population) and the saltwater crocodile (C. porosus). In the latter case the population of Papua New Guinea (which is being effectively managed) was excluded. The Mississippi alligator was downgraded from Appendix I to II, as this species, at least in Florida and Louisiana, is now locally abundant and can sustain a harvest; in addition there are a number of alligator farms.

- The biggest changes to the appendices were also those that provoked the least discussion - the <u>plants</u>. The CITES parties readily agreed to the addition of nearly 20 genera, including <u>Banksia</u> and many other Australian species. The Chilean population of the monkey puzzle tree was transferred to Appendix I.

---oooOooo---

The koala bear, in the past heavily reduced in numbers by the fur trade, is now protected in Australia. (Drawing: Peter Scott, © Fauna Preservation Society)

International Union for Conservation of Nature and Natural Resources
1110 Morges, Switzerland

Convention on International Trade in Endangered Species of Wild Fauna and Flora

Signed at Washington, D.C., on March 3, 1973

The Contracting States,

Recognizing that wild fauna and flora in their many beautiful and varied forms are an irreplaceable part of the natural systems of the earth which must be protected for this and the generations to come;

Conscious of the ever-growing value of wild fauna and flora from aesthetic, scientific, cultural, recreational and economic points of view;

Recognizing that peoples and States are and should be the best protectors of their own wild fauna and flora;

Recognizing, in addition, that international cooperation is essential for the protection of certain species of wild fauna and flora against over-exploitation through international trade;

Convinced of the urgency of taking appropriate measures to this end;

Have agreed as follows:

Article I
Definitions

For the purpose of the present Convention, unless the context otherwise requires:

(a) "Species" means any species, subspecies, or geographically separate population thereof;

(b) "Specimen" means:
  (i) any animal or plant, whether alive or dead;
  (ii) in the case of an animal: for species included in Appendices I and II, any readily recognizable part or derivative thereof; and for species included in Appendix III, any readily recognizable part or derivative thereof specified in Appendix III in relation to the species; and
  (iii) in the case of a plant: for species included in Appendix I, any readily recognizable part or derivative thereof; and for species included in Appendices II and III, any readily recognizable part or derivative thereof specified in Appendices II and III in relation to the species;

(c) "Trade" means export, re-export, import and introduction from the sea;

(d) "Re-export" means export of any specimen that has previously been imported;

(e) "Introduction from the sea" means transportation into a State of specimens of any species which were taken in the marine environment not under the jurisdiction of any State;

(f) "Scientific Authority" means a national scientific authority designated in accordance with Article IX;

(g) "Management Authority" means a national management authority designated in accordance with Article IX;

(h) "Party" means a State for which the present Convention has entered into force.

Article II
Fundamental Principles

1. Appendix I shall include all species threatened with extinction which are or may be affected by trade. Trade in specimens of these species must be subject to particularly strict regulation in order not to endanger further their survival and must only be authorized in exceptional circumstances.

2. Appendix II shall include:

(a) all species which although not necessarily now threatened with extinction may become so unless trade in specimens of such species is subject to strict regulation in order to avoid utilization incompatible with their survival; and

(b) other species which must be subject to regulation in order that trade in specimens of certain species referred to in sub-paragraph (a) of this paragraph may be brought under effective control.

3. Appendix III shall include all species which any Party identified as being subject to regulation within its jurisdiction for the purpose of preventing or restricting exploitation, and as needing the cooperation of other parties in the control of trade.

4. The Parties shall not allow trade in specimens of species included in Appendices I, II and III except in accordance with the provisions of the present Convention.

Article III
Regulation of Trade in Specimens of Species included in Appendix I

1. All trade in specimens of species included in Appendix I shall be in accordance with the provisions of this Article.

2. The export of any specimen of a species included in Appendix I shall require the prior grant and presentation of an export permit. An export permit shall only be granted when the following conditions have been met:

(a) a Scientific Authority of the State of export has advised that such export will not be detrimental to the survival of that species;

(b) a Management Authority of the State of export is satisfied that the specimen was not obtained in contravention of the laws of that State for the protection of fauna and flora;

(c) a Management Authority of the State of export is satisfied that any living specimen will be so prepared and shipped as to minimize the risk of injury, damage to health or cruel treatment; and

(d) a Management Authority of the State of export is satisfied that an import permit has been granted for the specimen.

3. The import of any specimen of a species included in Appendix I shall require the prior grant and presentation of an import permit and either an export permit or a re-export certi-

ficate. An import permit shall only be granted when the following conditions have been met:
 (a) a Scientific Authority of the State of import has advised that the import will be for purposes which are not detrimental to the survival of the species involved;
 (b) a Scientific Authority of the State of import is satisfied that the proposed recipient of a living specimen is suitably equipped to house and care for it; and
 (c) a Management Authority of the State of import is satisfied that the specimen is not to be used for primarily commercial purposes.

4. The re-export of any specimen of a species included in Appendix I shall require the prior grant and presentation of a re-export certificate. A re-export certificate shall only be granted when the following conditions have been met:
 (a) a Management Authority of the State of re-export is satisfied that the specimen was imported into that State in accordance with the provisions of the present Convention;
 (b) a Management Authority of the State of re-export is satisfied that any living specimen will be so prepared and shipped as to minimize the risk of injury, damage to health or cruel treatment; and
 (c) a Management Authority of the State of re-export is satisfied that an import permit has been granted for any living specimen.

5. The introduction from the sea of any specimen of a species included in Appendix I shall require the prior grant of a certificate from a Management Authority of the State of introduction. A certificate shall only be granted when the following conditions have been met:
 (a) a Scientific Authority of the State of introduction advises that the introduction will not be detrimental to the survival of the species involved;
 (b) a Management Authority of the State of introduction is satisfied that the proposed recipient of a living specimen is suitably equipped to house and care for it; and
 (c) a Management Authority of the State of introduction is satisfied that the specimen is not to be used for primarily commercial purposes.

Article IV
Regulation of Trade in Specimens of Species included in Appendix II

1. All trade in specimens of species included in Appendix II shall be in accordance with the provisions of this Article.

2. The export of any specimen of a species included in Appendix II shall require the prior grant and presentation of an export permit. An export permit shall only be granted when the following conditions have been met:
 (a) a Scientific Authority of the State of export has advised that such export will not be detrimental to the survival of that species;
 (b) a Management Authority of the State of export is satisfied that the specimen was not obtained in contravention of the laws of that State for the protection of fauna and flora; and
 (c) a Management Authority of the State of export is satisfied that any living specimen will be so prepared and shipped as to minimize the risk of injury, damage to health or cruel treatment.

3. A Scientific Authority in each Party shall monitor both the export permits granted by that State for specimens of species included in Appendix II and the actual exports of such specimens. Whenever a Scientific Authority determines that the export of specimens of any such species should be limited in order to maintain that species throughout its range at a level consistent with its role in the ecosystems in which it occurs and well above the level at which that species might become eligible for inclusion in Appendix I, the Scientific Authority shall advise the appropriate Management Authority of suitable measures to be taken to limit the grant of export permits for specimens of that species.

4. The import of any specimen of a species included in Appendix II shall require the prior presentation of either an export permit or a re-export certificate.

5. The re-export of any specimen of a species included in Appendix II shall require the prior grant and presentation of a re-export certificate. A re-export certificate shall only be granted when the following conditions have been met:
 (a) a Management Authority of the State of re-export is satisfied that the specimen was imported into that State in accordance with the provisions of the present Convention; and
 (b) a Management Authority of the State of re-export is satisfied that any living specimen will be so prepared and shipped as to minimize the risk of injury, damage to health or cruel treatment.

6. The introduction from the sea of any specimen of a species included in Appendix II shall require the prior grant of a certificate from a Management Authority of the State of introduction. A certificate shall only be granted when the following conditions have been met:
 (a) a Scientific Authority of the State of introduction advises that the introduction will not be detrimental to the survival of the species involved; and
 (b) a Management Authority of the State of introduction is satisfied that any living specimen will be so handled as to minimize the risk of injury, damage to health or cruel treatment.

7. Certificates referred to in paragraph 6 of this Article may be granted on the advice of a Scientific Authority, in consultation with other national scientific authorities or, when appropriate, international scientific authorities, in respect of periods not exceeding one year for total numbers of specimens to be introduced in such periods.

Article V
Regulation of Trade in Specimens of Species included in Appendix III

1. All trade in specimens of species included in Appendix III shall be in accordance with the provisions of this Article.

2. The export of any specimen of a species included in Appendix III from any State which has included that species in Appendix III shall require the prior grant and presentation of an export permit. An export permit shall only be granted when the following conditions have been met:
 (a) a Management Authority of the State of export is satisfied that the specimen was not obtained in contravention of the laws of that State for the protection of fauna and flora; and
 (b) a Management Authority of the State of export is satisfied that any living specimen will be so prepared and shipped as to minimize the risk of injury, damage to health or cruel treatment.

3. The import of any specimen of a species included in Appendix III shall require, except in circumstances to which paragraph 4 of this Article applies, the prior presentation of a certificate of origin and, where the import is from a State which has included that species in Appendix III, an export permit.

4. In the case of re-export, a certificate granted by the Management Authority of the State of re-export that the specimen was processed in that State or is being re-exported shall be accepted by the State of import as evidence that the provisions of the present Convention have been complied with in respect of the specimen concerned.

Article VI
Permits and Certificates

1. Permits and certificates granted under the provisions of Articles III, IV, and V shall be in accordance with the provisions of this Article.

2. An export permit shall contain the information specified in the model set forth in Appendix IV, and may only be used for export within a period of six months from the date on which it was granted.

3. Each permit or certificate shall contain the title of the present Convention, the name and any identifying stamp of the Management Authority granting it and a control number assigned by the Management Authority.

4. Any copies of a permit or certificate issued by a Management Authority shall be clearly marked as copies only and no such copy may be used in place of the original, except to the extent endorsed thereon.

5. A separate permit or certificate shall be required for each consignment of specimens.

6. A Management Authority of the State of import of any specimen shall cancel and retain the export permit or re-export certificate and any corresponding import permit presented in respect of the import of that specimen.

7. Where appropriate and feasible a Management Authority may affix a mark upon any specimen to assist in identifying the specimen. For these purposes "mark" means any indelible imprint, lead seal or other suitable means of identifying a specimen, designed in such a way as to render its imitation by unauthorized persons as difficult as possible.

Article VII
Exemptions and Other Special Provisions Relating to Trade

1. The provisions of Articles III, IV and V shall not apply to the transit or trans-shipment of specimens through or in the territory of a Party while the specimens remain in Customs control.

2. Where a Management Authority of the State of export or re-export is satisfied that a specimen was acquired before the provisions of the present Convention applied to that specimen, the provisions of Articles III, IV and V shall not apply to that specimen where the Management Authority issues a certificate to that effect.

3. The provisions of Articles III, IV and V shall not apply to specimens that are personal or household effects. This exemption shall not apply where:

   (a) in the case of specimens of a species included in Appendix I, they were acquired by the owner outside his State of usual residence, and are being imported into that State; or

   (b) in the case of specimens of species included in Appendix II:

      (i) they were acquired by the owner outside his State of usual residence and in a State where removal from the wild occurred;

      (ii) they are being imported into the owner's State of usual residence; and

      (iii) the State where removal from the wild occurred requires the prior grant of export permits before any export of such specimens;

   unless a Management Authority is satisfied that the specimens were acquired before the provisions of the present Convention applied to such specimens.

4. Specimens of an animal species included in Appendix I bred in captivity for commercial purpose, or of a plant species included in Appendix I artificially propagated for commercial purposes, shall be deemed to be specimens of species included in Appendix II.

5. Where a Management Authority of the State of export is satisfied that any specimen of an animal species was bred in captivity or any specimen of a plant species was artificially propagated, or is a part of such an animal or plant or was derived therefrom, a certificate by that Management Authority to that effect shall be accepted in lieu of any of the permits or certificates required under the provisions of Articles III, IV or V.

6. The provisions of Articles III, IV and V shall not apply to the non-commercial loan, donation or exchange between scientists or scientific institutions registered by a Management Authority of their State, of herbarium specimens, other preserved, dried or embedded museum specimens, and live plant material which carry a label issued or approved by a Management Authority.

7. A Management Authority of any State may waive the requirements of Articles III, IV and V and allow the movement without permits or certificates of specimens which form part of a travelling zoo, circus, menagerie, plant exhibition or other travelling exhibition provided that:

   (a) the exporter or importer registers full details of such specimens with that Management Authority;

   (b) the specimens are in either of the categories specified in paragraphs 2 or 5 of this Article; and

   (c) the Management Authority is satisfied that any living specimen will be so transported and cared for as to minimize the risk of injury, damage to health or cruel treatment.

Article VIII
Measures to be Taken by the Parties

1. The Parties shall take appropriate measures to enforce the provisions of the present Convention and to prohibit trade in specimens in violation thereof. These shall include measures:

   (a) to penalize trade in, or possession of, such specimens, or both; and

   (b) to provide for the confiscation or return to the State of export of such specimens.

2. In addition to the measures taken under paragraph 1 of this Article, a Party may, when it deems it necessary, provide for any method of internal reimbursement for expenses incurred as a result of the confiscation of a specimen traded in violation of the measures taken in the application of the provisions of the present Convention.

3. As far as possible, the Parties shall ensure that specimens shall pass through any formalities required for trade with a minimum of delay. To facilitate such passage, a Party may designate ports of exit and ports of entry at which specimens must be presented for clearance. The Parties shall ensure further that all living specimens, during any period of transit, holding or shipment, are properly cared for so as to minimize the risk of injury, damage to health or cruel treatment.

4. Where a living specimen is confiscated as a result of measures referred to in paragraph 1 of this Article:

   (a) the specimen shall be entrusted to a Management Authority of the State of confiscation;

   (b) the Management Authority shall, after consultation with the State of export, return the specimen to that State at the expense of that State, or to a rescue centre or such other place as the Management Authority deems appropriate and consistent with the purposes of the present Convention; and

   (c) the Management Authority may obtain the advice of a Scientific Authority, or may, whenever it considers it desirable, consult the Secretariat in order to facilitate the decision under subparagraph (b) of this paragraph, including the choice of a rescue centre or other place.

5. A rescue centre as referred to in paragraph 4 of this Article means an institution designated by a Management Authority to look after the welfare of living specimens, particularly those that have been confiscated.

6. Each Party shall maintain records of trade in specimens of species included in Appendices I, II and III which shall cover:

   (a) the names and addresses of exporters and importers; and

   (b) the number and type of permits and certificates granted; the States with which such trade occurred; the numbers or quantities and types of specimens, names of species as included in Appendices I, II and III and, where applicable, the size and sex of the specimens in question.

7. Each Party shall prepare periodic reports on its implementation of the present Convention and shall transmit to the Secretariat:

   (a) an annual report containing a summary of the information specified in sub-paragraph (b) of paragraph 6 of this Article; and

   (b) a biennial report on legislative, regulatory and administrative measures taken to enforce the provisions of the present Convention.

8. The information referred to in paragraph 7 of this Article shall be available to the public where this is not inconsistent with the law of the Party concerned.

Article IX
Management and Scientific Authorities

1. Each Party shall designate for the purpose of the present Convention:

   (a) one or more Management Authorities competent to grant permits or certificates on behalf of that Party; and

   (b) one or more Scientific Authorities.

2. A State depositing an instrument of ratification, acceptance, approval or accession shall at that time inform the Depositary Government of the name and address of the Management Authority authorized to communicate with other Parties and with the Secretariat.

3. Any changes in the designations or authorizations under the provisions of this Article shall be communicated by the Party concerned to the Secretariat for transmission to all other Parties.

4. Any Management Authority referred to in paragraph 2 of this Article shall if so requested by the Secretariat or the Management Authority of another Party, communicate to it impression of stamps, seals or other devices used to authenticate permits or certificates.

Article X
Trade with States not Party to the Convention

Where export or re-export is to, or import is from, a State not a party to the present Convention, comparable documentation issued by the competent authorities in that State which substantially conforms with the requirements of the present Convention for permits and certificates may by accepted in lieu thereof by any Party.

Article XV
Amendments to Appendices I and II

1. The following provisions shall apply in relation to amendments to Appendices I and II at meetings of the Conference of the Parties:

(a) Any Party may propose an amendment to Appendix I or II for consideration at the next meeting. The text of the proposed amendment shall be communicated to the Secretariat at least 150 days before the meeting. The Secretariat shall consult the other Parties and interested bodies on the amendment in accordance with the provisions of sub-paragraph (b) and (c) of paragraph 2 of this Article and shall communicate the response to all Parties not later than 30 days before the meeting.

(b) Amendments shall be adopted by a two-thirds majority of Parties present and voting. For these purposes "Parties present and voting" means Parties present and casting an affirmative or negative vote. Parties abstaining from voting shall not be counted among the two-thirds required for adopting an amendment.

(c) Amendments adopted at a meeting shall enter into force 90 days after that meeting for all Parties except those which make a reservation in accordance with paragraph 3 of this Article.

2. The following provisions shall apply in relation to amendments to Appendices I and II between meetings of the Conference of the Parties:

(a) Any Party may propose an amendment to Appendix I or II for consideration between meetings by the postal procedures set forth in this paragraph.

(b) For marine species, the Secretariat shall, upon receiving the text of the proposed amendment, immediately communicate it to the Parties. It shall also consult inter-governmental bodies having a function in relation to those species especially with a view to obtaining scientific data these bodies may be able to provide and to ensuring coordination with any conservation measures enforced by such bodies. The Secretariat shall communicate the views expressed and data provided by these bodies and its own findings and recommendations to the Parties as soon as possible.

(c) For species other than marine species, the Secretariat shall, upon receiving the text of the proposed amendment, immediately communicate it to the Parties, and, as soon as possible thereafter, its own recommendations.

(d) Any Party may, within 60 days of the date on which the Secretariat communicated its recommendations to the Parties under sub-paragraphs (b) or (c) of this paragraph, transmit to the Secretariat any comments on the proposed amendment together with any relevant scintific data and information.

(e) The Secretariat shall communicate the replies received together with its own recommendations to the Parties as soon as possible.

(f) If no objection to the proposed amendment is received by the Secretariat within 30 days of the date the replies and recommendations were communicated under the provisions of sub-paragraph (e) of this paragraph, the amendment shall enter into force 90 days later for all Parties except those which make a reservation in accordance with paragraph 3 of this Article.

(g) If an objection by any Party is received by the Secretariat, the proposed amendment shall be submitted to a postal vote in accordance with the provisions of sub-paragraphs (h), (i) and (j) of this paragraph.

(h) The Secretariat shall notify the Parties that notification of objection has been received.

(i) Unless the Secretariat receives the votes for, against or in abstention from at least one-half of the Parties within 60 days of the date of notification under sub-paragraph (h) of this paragraph, the proposed amendment shall be referred to the next meeting of the Conference for further consideration.

(j) Provided that votes are received from one-half of the Parties, the amendment shall be adopted by a two-thirds majority of Parties casting an affirmative or negative vote.

(k) The Secretariat shall notify all Parties of the result of the vote.

(l) If the proposed amendment is adopted it shall enter into force 90 days after the date of the notification by the Secretariat of its acceptance for all Parties except those which make a reservation in accordance with paragraph 3 of this Article.

3. During the period of 90 days provided for by sub-paragraph (c) of paragraph 1 or sub-paragraph (l) of paragraph 2 of this Article any Party may by notification in writing to the Depositary Government make a reservation with respect to the amendment. Until such reservation is withdrawn the Party shall be treated as a State not a Party to the present Convention with respect to trade in the species concerned.

Article XVI
Appendix III and Amendments thereto

1. Any party may at any time submit to the Secretariat a list of species which it identifies as being subject to regulation within its jurisdiction for the purpose mentioned in paragraph 3 of Article II. Appendix III shall include the names of the Parties submitting the species for inclusion therein, the scientific names of the species so submitted, and any parts or derivatives of the animals or plants concerned that are specified in relation to the species for the purposes of sub-paragraph (b) of Article I.

2. Each list submitted under the provisions of paragraph 1 of this Article shall be communicated to the Parties by the Secretariat as soon as possible after receiving it. The list shall take effect as part of Appendix III 90 days after the date of such communication. At any time after the communication of such list, any Party may by notification in writing to the Depositary Government enter a reservation with respect to any species or any parts or derivatives, and until such reservation is withdrawn, the State shall be treated as a State not a Party to the present Convention with respect to trade in the species or part or derivative concerned.

3. A Party which has submitted a species for inclusion in Appendix III may withdraw it at any time by notification to the Secretariat which shall communicate the withdrawal to all Parties. The withdrawal shall take effect 30 days after the date of such communication.

4. Any Party submitting a list under the provisions of paragraph 1 of this Article shall submit to the Secretariat a copy of all domestic laws and regulations applicable to the protection of such species, together with any interpretations which the Party may deem appropriate or the Secretariat may request. The Party shall, for as long as the species in questions is included in Appendix III, submit any amendment of such laws and regulations or any new interpretations as they are adopted.

Article XVII
Amendment of the Convention

1. An extraordinary meeting of the Conference of the Parties shall be convened by the Secretariat on the written request of at least one-third of the Parties to consider and adopt amendments to the present Convention. Such amendments shall be adopted by a two-thirds majority of Parties present and voting. For these purposes "Parties present and voting" means Parties present and casting an affirmative or negative vote. Parties abstaining from voting shall not be counted among the two-thirds required for adopting an amendment.

2. The text of any proposed amendment shall be communicated by the Secretariat to all Parties at least 90 days before the meeting.

3. An amendment shall enter into force for the Parties which have accepted it 60 days after two-thirds of the Parties have deposited an instrument of acceptance of the amendment with the Depositary Government. Thereafter, the amendment shall enter into force for any other Party 60 days after that Party deposits its instrument of acceptance of the amendment.

Article XVIII
Resolution of Disputes

1. Any dispute which may arise between two or more Parties with respect to the interpretation or application of the provisions of the present Convention shall be subject to negotiation between the Parties involved in the dispute.

2. If the dispute cannot be resolved in accordance with paragraph 1 of this Article, the Parties may, by mutual consent, submit the dispute to arbitration, in particular that of the Permanent Court of Arbitration at The Hague and the Parties submitting the dispute shall be bound by the arbitral decision.

Article XIX
Signature

The present Convention shall be open for signature at Washington until 30th April 1973 and thereafter at Berne until 31st December 1974.

Article XI
Conference of the Parties

1. The Secretariat shall call a meeting of the Conference of the Parties not later than two years after the entry into force of the present Convention.

2. Thereafter the Secretariat shall convene regular meetings at least once every two years, unless the Conference decides otherwise, and extraordinary meetings at any time on the written request of at least one-third of the Parties.

3. At meetings, whether regular or extraordinary, the Parties shall review the implementation of the present Convention and may:

   (a) make such provision as may be necessary to enable the Secretariat to carry out its duties;

   (b) consider and adopt amendements to Appendices I and II in accordance with Article XV;

   (c) review the progress made towards the restoration and conservation of the species included in Appendices I, II and III;

   (d) receive and consider any reports presented by the Secretariat or by any Party; and

   (e) where appropriate, make recommendations for improving the effectiveness of the present Convention.

4. At each regular meeting, the Parties may determine the time and venue of the next regular meeting to be held in accordance with the provisions of paragraph 2 of this Article.

5. At any meeting, the Parties may determine and adopt rules of procedure for the meeting.

6. The United Nations, its Specialized Agencies and the International Atomic Energy Agency, as well as any State not a Party to the present Convention, may be represented at meetings of the Conference by observers, who shall have the right to participate but not to vote.

7. Any body or agency technically qualified in protection, conservation or management of wild fauna and flora, in the following catagories, which has informed the Secretariat of its desire to be represented at meetings of the Conference by observers, shall be admitted unless at least one-third of the Parties present object:

   (a) international agencies or bodies, either governmental or non-governmental, and national governmental agencies and bodies; and

   (b) national non-governmental agencies or bodies which have been approved for this purpose by the State in which they are located.

Once admitted, these observers shall have the right to participate but not to vote.

Article XII
The Secretariat

1. Upon entry into force of the present Convention, a Secretariat shall be provided by the Executive Director of the United Nations Environment Programme. To the extent and in the manner he considers appropriate, he may be assisted by suitable inter-governmental or non-governmental, international or national agencies and bodies technically qualified in protection, conservation and management of wild fauna and flora.

2. The functions of the Secretariat shall be:

   (a) to arrange for and service meetings of the Parties;

   (b) to perform the functions entrusted to it under the provisions of Articles XV and XVI of the present Convention;

   (c) to undertake scientific and technical studies in accordance with programmes authorized by the Conference of the Parties as will contribute to the implementation of the present Convention, including studies concerning standards for appropriate preparation and shipment of living specimens and the means of identifying specimens;

   (d) to study the reports of Parties and to request from Parties such further information with respect thereto as it deems necessary to ensure implementation of the present Convention;

   (e) to invite the attention of the Parties to any matter pertaining to the aims of the present Convention;

   (f) to publish periodically and distribute to the Parties current editions of Appendices I, II and III together with any information which will facilitate identification of specimens of species included in those Appendices.

   (g) to prepare annual reports to the Parties on its work and on the implementation of the present Convention and such other reports as meetings of the Parties may request;

   (h) to make recommendations for the implementation of the aims and provisions of the present Convention, including the exchange of information of a scientific or technical nature;

   (i) to perform any other function as may be entrusted to it by the Parties.

Article XIII
International Measures

1. When the Secretariat in the light of information received is satisfied that any species included in Appendices I or II is being affected adversely by trade in specimens of that species or that the provisions of the present Convention are not being effectively implemented, it shall communicate such information to the authorized Management Authority of the Party or Parties concerned.

2. When any Party receives a communication as indicated in paragraph 1 of this Article, it shall, as soon as possible, inform the Secretariat of any relevant facts insofar as its laws permit and, where appropriate, propose remedial action. Where the Party considers that an inquiry is desirable, such inquiry may be carried out by one or more persons expressly authorized by the Party.

3. The information provided by the Party or resulting from any inquiry as specified in paragraph 2 of this Article shall be reviewed by the next Conference of the Parties which may make whatever recommendations it deems appropriate.

Article XIV
Effect on Domestic Legislation and International Conventions

1. The provisions of the present Convention shall in no way affect the right of Parties to adopt:

   (a) stricter domestic measures regarding the conditions for trade, taking, possession or transport of specimens of species included in Appendices I, II and III, or the complete prohibition thereof; or

   (b) domestic measures restricting or prohibiting trade, taking, possession, or transport of species not included in Appendices I, II or III.

2. The provisions of the present Convention shall in no way affect the provisions of any domestic measures or the obligations of Parties deriving from any treaty, convention; or international agreement relating to other aspects of trade, taking, possession, or transport of specimens which is in force or subsequently may enter into force for any Party including any measure pertaining to the Customs, public health, veterinary or plant quarantine fields.

3. The provisions of the present Convention shall in no way affect the provisions of, or the obligations deriving from, any treaty, convention or international agreement concluded or which may be concluded between States creating a union or regional trade agreement establishing or maintaining a common external customs control and removing customs control between the parties thereto insofar as they relate to trade among the States members of that union agreement.

4. A State Party to the present Convention, which is also a party to any other treaty, convention or international agreement which is in force at the time of the coming into force of the present Convention and under the provisions of which protection is afforded to marine species included in Appendix II, shall be relieved of the obligation imposed on it under the provisions of the present Convention with respect to trade in specimens of species included in Appendix II that are taken by ships registered in that State and in accordance with the provisions of such other treaty, convention or international agreement.

5. Notwithstanding the provisions of Articles III, IV and V, any export of a specimen taken in accordance with paragraph 4 of this Article shall only require a certificate from a Management Authority of the State of introduction to the effect that the specimen was taken in accordance with the provisions of the other treaty, convention or international agreement in question.

6. Nothing in the present Convention shall prejudice the codification and development of the law of the sea by the United Nations Conference on the Law of the Sea convened pursuant to Resolution 2750 C (XXV) of the General Assembly of the United Nations nor the present or future claims and legal views of any State concerning the law of the sea and the nature and extent of coastal and flag State jurisdiction.

Article XX
Ratification, Acceptance, Approval

The present Convention shall be subject to ratification, acceptance or approval. Instruments of ratification, acceptance or approval shall be deposited with the Government of the Swiss Confederation which shall be the Depositary Government.

Article XXI
Accession

The present Convention shall be open indefinitely for accession. Instruments of accession shall be deposited with the Depositary Government.

Article XXII
Entry into Force

1. The present Convention shall enter into force 90 days after the date of deposit of the tenth instrument of ratification, acceptance, approval or accession, with the Depositary Government.
2. For each State which ratifies, accepts or approves the present Convention or accedes thereto after the deposit of the tenth instrument of ratification, acceptance, approval or accession, the present Convention shall enter into force 90 days after the deposit by such State of its instrument of ratification, acceptance, approval or accession.

Article XXIII
Reservations

1. The provisions of the present Convention shall not be subject to general reservations. Specific reservations may be entered in accordance with the provisions of this Article and Articles XV and XVI.
2. Any State may, on depositing its instrument of ratification, acceptance, approval or accession, enter a specific reservation with regard to:

(a) any species included in Appendix I, II or III; or
(b) any parts or derivatives specified in relation to a species concluded in Appendix III.

3. Until a Party withdraws its reservation entered under the provisions of this Article, it shall be treated as a State not a party to the present Convention with respect to trade in the particular species or parts or derivatives specified in such reservation.

Article XXIV
Denunciation

Any Party may denounce the present Convention by written notification to the Depositary Government at any time. The denunciation shall take effect twelve months after the Depositary Government has received the notification.

Article XXV
Depositary

1. The original of the present Convention, in the Chinese, English, French, Russian and Spanish languages, each version being equally authentic, shall be deposited with the Depositary Government, which shall transmit certified copies thereof to all States that have signed it or deposited instruments of accession to it.
2. The Depositary Government shall inform all signatory and acceding States and the Secretariat of signatures, deposit of instruments of ratification, acceptance, approval or accession, entry into force of the present Convention, amendments thereto, entry and withdrawal of reservations and notifications of denunciation.
3. As soon as the present Convention enters into force, a certified copy thereof shall be transmitted by the Depositary Government to the Secretariat of the United Nations for registration and publication in accordance with Article 102 of the Charter of the United Nations.

In witness whereof the undersigned Plenipotentiaries, being duly authorized to that effect, have signed the present Convention.

Done at Washington this third day of March, One Thousand Nine Hundred and Seventy-three.

ANNEX 2

CITES

APPENDICES I AND II

as at 28 June 1979

INTERPRETATION

1. Species included in these appendices are referred to:
   a) by the name of the species; or
   b) as being all of the species included in a higher taxon or deisgnated part thereof.

2. The abbreviation "spp" is used to denote all species of a higher taxon.

3. Other references to taxa higher than species are for the purposes of information or classification only.

4. The abbreviation "p.e." is used to denote species which are possibly extinct.

5. An asterisk (*) placed against the name of a species or higher taxon indicates that one or more geographically separate populations, subspecies or species of that species or taxon are included in Appendix I and that these populations, subspecies or species are excluded from Appendix II.

6. Two asterisks (**) placed against the name of a species or higher taxon indicate that one or more geographically separate populations, subspecies or species of that species or taxon are included in Appendix II and that these populations, subspecies or species are excluded from Appendix I.

7. The symbol (+) followed by a number placed against the name of a species or higher taxon denotes that only designated geographically separate populations, subspecies or species of that species or taxon are included in the appendix concerned, as follows:

   +201 Population of South America
   +202 (A) North Pacific stock
        (B) Stock in area from 0 degree longitude to 70 degrees east longitude, from the equator to the Antarctic continent
   +203 Populations of Bhutan, India, Nepal and Pakistan
   +204 Italian population
   +205 All North American subspecies
   +206 Asian population
   +207 Indian population
   +208 Australian population
   +209 Himalayan population
   +210 Population of the United States of America
   +211 All New Zealand species
   +212 Population of Chile
   +213 All species of the family in the Americas
   +214 Australian populations

8. The symbol (-) followed by a number placed against the name of a species or higher taxon denotes that designated geographically separate populations, subspecies, species, groups of species or families of that species or taxon are excluded from the appendix concerned, as follows:

   -101 (A) Stock in North Atlantic off Iceland
        (B) Stock in North Atlantic off Newfoundland
        (C) Stock in area from 40 degrees south latitude to Antarctic Continent, from 120 degrees west longitude to 60 degrees west longitude
   -102 Populations of Bhutan, India, Nepal and Pakistan
   -103 Panthera tigris altaica (=amurensis)
   -104 Australian population
   -105 Cathartidae
   -106 Population of the United States of America
   -107 Australian population
   -108 Population of Papua New Guinea
   -109 Population of Chile
   -110 All species which are not succulent

9. Any plant, whether alive or dead, as well as any readily recognisable part or derivative of a plant of a species or higher taxon included in Appendix II are covered by the provisions of the Convention, unless the symbol (≠) followed by a number is placed against the name of that species or taxon. In such a case, only the plant, whether alive or dead, and the parts or derivatives designated as follows are concerned:

   ≠ 1 designates roots
   ≠ 2 designates timber
   ≠ 3 designates trunks

APPENDIX I

MAMMALS

Bettongia spp (Rat-kangaroos)
Caloprymnus campestris p.e. (Desert rat-kangaroo)

Lagorchestes hirsutus (Western hare-wallaby)
Lagostrophus fasciatus (Banded hare-wallaby)
Onychogalea frenata (Merrin)
Onychogalea lunata (Wurrung)

Lasiorhinus krefftii (Queensland hairy-nosed wombat)
Chaeropus ecaudatus p.e. (Pig-footed bandicoot)
Macrotis lagotis (Bilby)
Macrotis leucura (Yallara)
Perameles bougainville (Marl)
Sminthopsis longicaudata (Long-tailed dunnart)
Sminthopsis psammophila (Sandhill dunnart)
Thylacinus cynocephalus (Thylacine)

Allocebus spp (Hairy-eared dwarf lemurs)
Cheirogaleus spp (Fat-tailed dwarf lemurs)
Hapalemur spp (Gentle lemurs)
Lemur spp (Lemurs)
Lepilemur spp (Sportive lemurs)
Microcebus spp (Mouse lemurs)
Phaner spp (Fork-marked mouse lemurs)

Avahi spp (Woolly indris)
Indri spp (Indris)
Propithecus spp (Sifakas)

Daubentonia madagascariensis (Aye-aye)

Callimico goeldii (Goeldi's marmoset)
Callithrix aurita (White-eared marmoset)
Callithrix flaviceps (Buff-headed marmoset)
Leontopithecus (Leontideus) spp (Golden tamarins)
Saguinus bicolor (Bare-faced tamarin)
Saguinus leucopus (White-footed tamarin)
Saguinus oedipus (Cotton-headed tamarin)

Alouatta palliata (villosa) (Mantled howler)
Ateles geoffroyi frontatus (Black-browed spider monkey)
Ateles geoffroyi panamensis (Red spider monkey)
Brachyteles arachnoides (Woolly spider monkey)
Cacajao spp (Uakaris)
Chiropotes albinasus (White-nosed saki)
Saimiri oerstedii (Red-backed squirrel monkey)
Cercocebus galeritus galeritus (Tana River mangabey)
Colobus badius kirkii (Zanzibar red colobus)
Colobus badius rufomitratus (Tana River red colobus)
Macaca silenus (Lion-tailed macaque)
Nasalis larvatus (Proboscis monkey)
Presbytis entellus (Entellus langur)
Presbytis geei (Golden langur)
Presbytis pileatus (Capped langur)
Presbytis potenziani (Mentawai leaf monkey)
Pygathrix nemaus (Douc langur)
Simias concolor (Pig-tailed langur)

Hylobates spp (Gibbons)
Symphalangus syndactylus (Siamang)

Pongidae spp (Gorilla, orang-utan and chimpanzees)

Priodontes giganteus (= maximus) (Giant armadillo)

Manis temmincki (Cape pangolin)

Caprolagus hispidus (Hispid hare)

Romerolagus diazi (Volcano rabbit)

APPENDIX II

Zaglossus spp (New Guinea echidnas)

Dendrolagus bennettianus (Bennett's tree kangaroo)
Dendrolagus lumholtzi (Lumholtz's tree kangaroo)
Dendrolagus inustus (Grizzled tree kangaroo)
Dendrolagus ursinus (Black tree kangaroo)

Phalanger maculatus (Spotted cuscus)
Phalanger orientalis (Grey cuscus)
Burramys parvus (Mountain pygmy possum)

Erinaceus frontalis (Cape hedgehog)

All primate species*

Myrmecophaga tridactyla (Giant anteater)
Tamandua tetradactyla chapadensis
 (Mato Grosso tamandua)
Bradypus boliviensis (Bolivian three-toed sloth)
Manis crassicaudata (Indian pangolin)
Manis javanica (Malayan pangolin)
Manis pentadactyla (Chinese pangolin)

Nesolagus netscheri (Sumatra short-eared rabbit)

APPENDIX I

MAMMALS (contd)

Cynomys mexicanus (Mexican prairie dog)

Leporillus conditor (Stick-nest rat)

Pseudomys fumeus (Smokey mouse)
Pseudomys praeconis (Shark Bay mouse)

Xeromys myoides (False water rat)
Zyzomys pedunculatus (Macdonnell Range rock-rat)

Chinchilla spp +201 (Chinchillas)

Lipotes vexillifer (White flag dolphin)
Platanista gangetica (Ganges susu)
Platanista indi (Indus susu)
Sotalia spp (South American river dolphins)
Sousa spp (Hump-backed dolphins)
Neophocaena phocaenoides (Finless porpoise)
Phocoena sinus (Cochito)
Eschrichtius robustus (glaucus) (Grey whale)
Balaenoptera borealis ** +202 (Sei whale)
Balaenoptera musculus (Blue whale)
Balaenoptera physalus ** - 101 (Fin whale)
Megaptera novaeangliae (Humpback whale)
Balaena mysticetus (Bowhead whale)
Eubalaena spp (Right whales)

Canis lupus ** +203 (Grey wolf)

Speothos venaticus (Bush dog)

Vulpes velox hebes (Northern swift fox)

Helarctos malayanus (Sun bear)
Selenarctos thibetanus (Asiatic black bear)
Tremarctos ornatus (Spectacled bear)
Ursus arctos ** +204
Ursus arctos isabellinus (Himalayan brown bear)
Ursus arctos nelsoni (Mexican grizzly bear)
Ursus arctos pruinosus (Tibetan brown bear)

Aonyx microdon (Cameroon clawless otter)

Enhydra lutris nereis (Southern sea otter)
Lutra felina (Marine otter)
Lutra longicaudis (platensis/annectens)
(La Plata otter)
Lutra lutra (European otter)
Lutra provocax (Southern river otter)

Mustela nigripes (Black-footed ferret)
Pteronura brasiliensis (Giant otter)

Prionodon pardicolor (Spotted linsang)
Hyaena brunnea (Brown hyaena)

Acinonyx jubatus (Cheetah)
Felis bengalensis bengalensis (Indian leopard cat)
Felis caracal ** +206 (Caracal)
Felis concolor coryi (Florida puma)
Felis concolor costaricensis (Costa Rican puma)
Felis concolor cougar (Eastern puma)
Felis jacobita (Mountain cat)
Felis marmorata (Marbled cat)
Felis nigripes (Black-footed cat)
Felis pardalis mearnsi (Costa Rican ocelot)

APPENDIX II

Lariscus hosei (Four-striped ground squirrel)
Ratufa spp (Giant squirrels)
Dipodomys phillipsii phillipsii
  (Phillips's kangaroo rat)
Notomys spp (Hopping mice)

Pseudomys shortridgei (Shortridge's native mouse)

Cetacea spp (Whales, dolphins, porpoises)

Canis lupus * -102 (Grey wolf)
Chrysocyon brachyurus (Maned wolf)
Cuon alpinus (Dhole)
Dusicyon culpaeus (Culpeo fox)
Dusycion fulvipes (Chiloe fox)
Dusycion griseus (Chico grey fox)

Vulpes cana (Afghan fox)

Ursus arctos * +205

Ursus (Thalarctos)maritimus (Polar bear)
Ailurus fulgens (Lesser panda)

Conepatus humboldti (Patagonian skunk)

Lutrinae spp * (Otters)

Cryptoprocta ferox (Fossa)
Cynogale bennetti (Otter civet)
Eupleres goudotii (Falanouc)
Eupleres major (Malagasy mongoose)
Fossa fossa (Malagasy civet)
Hemigalus derbyanus (Banded palm civet)
Prionodon linsang (Banded linsang)

Felidae spp*(Cats)

APPENDIX I

MAMMALS (contd)

Felis pardalis mitis (Brazilian ocelot)
Felis planiceps (Flat-headed cat)
Felis rubiginosa ** +207 (Rusty-spotted cat)
Felis (Lynx) rufa escuinapae (Mexican bobcat)
Felis temmincki (Asiatic golden cat)
Felis tigrina oncilla (Costa Rican tiger cat)
Felis wiedii nicaraguae (Nicaraguan margay)
Felis wiedii salvinia (Guatemalan margay)
Felis yagouaroundi cacomitli (Tamaulipas jaguarundi)
Felis yagouaroundi fossata (Yucatan jaguarundi)
Felis yagouaroundi panamensis (Panama jaguarundi)
Felis yagouaroundi tolteca (Sinaloa jaguarundi)
Neofelis nebulosa (Clouded leopard)
Panthera leo persica (Asiatic lion)
Panthera onca (Jaguar)
Panthera pardus (Leopard)
Panthera tigris ** -103 (Tiger)
Panthera uncia (Snow leopard)

Arctocephalus townsendi (Guadalupe fur seal)

Monachus spp (Monk seals)

Elephas maximus (Asian elephant)

Dugong dugon ** -104 (Dugong)
Trichechus inunguis (South American manatee)
Trichechus manatus (North American manatee)

Equus grevyi (Grevy's zebra)

Equus hemionus hemionus (Mongolian wild ass)
Equus hemionus khur (Indian wild ass)
Equus przewalskii (Przewalski's horse)

Equus zebra zebra (Cape mountain zebra)
Tapirus bairdii (Central American tapir)
Tapirus indicus (Malayan tapir)
Tapirus pinchaque (Mountain tapir)

Rhinocerotidae spp (Rhinoceroses)
Babyrousa babyrussa (Babirusa)
Sus salvanius (Pygmy hog)

Vicugna vicugna (Vicuna)
Axis (Hyelaphus) calamianensis (Calamian deer)
Axis (Hyelaphus) khuli (Kuhl's deer)
Axis (Hyelaphus) porcinus annamiticus (Ganges hog deer)
Blastocerus dichotomus (Marsh deer)
Cervus duvauceli (Swamp deer)

Cervus elaphus hanglu (Kashmir red deer)
Cervus eldi (Brow-antlered deer)
Dama mesopotamica (Persian fallow deer)
Hippocamelus antisensis (North Andean huemal)
Hippocamelus bisulcus (South Andean huemal)

Moschus moschiferus ** +209 (Himalayan musk deer)
Ozotoceros bezoarticus (Pampas deer)

Pudu pudu (Southern pudu)

Antilocapra americana peninsularis
  (Sonoran pronghorn)
Antilocapra americana sonoriensis
  (Lower California pronghorn)

Bison bison athabascae (Wood bison)
Bos gaurus (Gaur)
Bos (grunniens) mutus (Wild yak)
Bubalus (Anoa) depressicornis (Lowland anoa)
Bubalus (Anoa) mindorensis (Tamaraw)
Bubalus (Anoa) quarlesi (Mountain anoa)

Capra falconeri chiltanensis (Chiltan markhor)
Capra falconeri jerdoni (Straight-horned markhor)
Capra falconeri megaceros (Kabul markhor)
Capricornis sumatraensis (Serow)

APPENDIX II

Arctocephalus spp* (Fur seals)

Mirounga angustirostris (Northern elephant seal)
Mirounga leonina (Southern elephant seal)

Orycteropus afer (Aardvark)

Loxodonta africana (African elephant)
Dugong dugon * +208 (Dugong)

Trichechus senegalensis (West African manatee)

Equus hemionus * (Asiatic wild ass)

Equus zebra hartmannae (Hartmann's mountain zebra)

Tapirus terrestris (South American tapir)

Choeropsis liberiensis (Pygmy hippopotamus)
Lama guanicoe (Guanaco)

Cervus elaphus bactrianus (Bactrian red deer)

Moschus spp * (Musk deer)

Pudu mephistophiles (Northern pudu)

Antilocapra americana mexicana (Mexican pronghorn)

Addax nasomaculatus (Addax)

Capra falconeri* (Markhor)

APPENDIX I

MAMMALS (contd)

Damaliscus dorcas dorcas (Bontebok)
Hippotragus niger variani (Giant sable antelope)
Nemorhaedus goral (Goral)
Novibos (Bos) sauveli (Kouprey)
Oryx leucoryx (Arabian oryx)
Ovis ammon hodgsoni (Nyan)
Ovis orientalis ophion (Cyprus mouflon)
Ovis vignei (Urial)
Pantholops hodgsoni (Chiru)
Rupicapra rupicapra ornata (Abruzzi chamois)

BIRDS

Pterocnemia pennata (Lesser rhea)

Tinamus solitarius (Solitary tinamou)

Podilymbus gigas (Atitlan grebe)
Diomedea albatrus (Short-tailed albatross)

Sula abbotti (Abbott's booby)
Fregata andrewsi (Christmas Island frigate bird)
Ciconia ciconia boyciana (Oriental white stork)

Geronticus eremita (Northern bald ibis)
Nipponia nippon (Japanese crested ibis)

Anas aucklandica nesiotis (Campbell Is. brown teal)

Anas laysanensis (Laysan duck)
Anas oustaleti (Marianas duck)

Branta canadensis leucopareia
 (Aleutian Canada goose)

Branta sandvicensis (Hawaiian goose)
Cairina scutulata (White-winged wood duck)

Rhodonessa caryophyllacea (Pink-headed duck)

Gymnogyps californianus (California condor)
Vultur gryphus (Andean condor)
Aquila heliaca (Imperial eagle)
Chondrohierax wilsonii (Cuban hook-billed kite)
Haliaeetus albicilla (White-tailed eagle)
Haliaeetus leucocephalus (Bald eagle)
Harpia harpyja (South American harpy eagle)
Pithecophaga jefferyi (Philippine eagle)

APPENDIX II

Cephalophus monticola (Blue duiker)

Kobus leche (Lechwe)

Oryx (tao) dammah (Scimitar-horned oryx)
Ovis ammon* (Argali)
Ovis canadensis (Bighorn sheep)

Rhea americana albescens (Argentine greater rhea)
Rhynchotus rufescens maculicollis
 (Bolivian rufous tinamou)
Rhynchotus rufescens pallescens
 (Argentine rufous tinamou)
Rhynchotus rufescens rufescens
 (Brazilian rufous tinamou)

Spheniscus demersus (Black-footed penguin)

Pelecanus crispus (Dalmatian pelican)

Ciconia nigra (Black stork)
Geronticus calvus (Southern bald ibis)

Platalea leucorodia (White spoonbill)
Phoenicoparrus andinus (Andean flamingo)
Phoenicoparrus jamesi (James' flamingo)
Phoenicoparrus ruber chilensis (Chilean flamingo)
Phoenicoparrus ruber ruber (Caribbean flamingo)

Anas aucklandica aucklandica
 (Auckland Is. brown teal)
Anas aucklandica chlorotis
 (New Zealand brown teal)
Anas bernieri (Madagascar teal)

Anser albifrons gambelli
 (Tule white-fronted goose)

Branta ruficollis (Red-breasted goose)

Coscoroba coscoroba (Coscoroba swan)
Cygnus bewickii jankowskii
 (Eastern Bewick's swan)
Cygnus melancoryphus (Black-necked swan)
Dendrocygna arborea (Black-billed whistling duck)

Sarkidiornis melanotos (Comb duck)

Falconiformes spp* -105 (Birds of prey)

APPENDIX I

BIRDS (contd)

Falco araea (Seychelles kestrel)
Falco newtoni aldabranus (Aldabra kestrel)
Falco peregrinus (pelegrinoides/babylonicus)
 (Peregrine falcon)
Falco punctatus (Mauritius kestrel)
Falco rusticolus (Gyr falcon)
Macrocephalon maleo (Maleo fowl)

Crax blumenbachii (Red-billed curassow)
Mitu mitu mitu (Greater razor-billed curassow)
Oreophasis derbianus (Horned guan)
Pipile jacutinga (Black-fronted piping guan)
Pipile pipile pipile (Trinidad blue-throated curassow)

Tympanuchus cupido attwateri
 (Attwater's prairie chicken)

Catreus wallichii (Cheer pheasant)
Colinus virginianus ridgwayi (Masked bobwhite)
Crossoptilon crossoptilon (White eared pheasant)
Crossoptilon mantchuricum (Brown eared pheasant)

Lophophorus impejanus (Himalayan monal)
Lophophorus lhuysii (Chinese monal)
Lophophorus sclateri (Sclater's monal)
Lophura edwardsi (Edwards's pheasant)
Lophura imperialis (Imperial pheasant)
Lophura swinhoii (Swinhoe's pheasant)

Polyplectron emphanum (Palawan peacock-pheasant)

Syrmaticus ellioti (Elliot's pheasant)
Syrmaticus humiae (Hume's pheasant)
Syrmaticus mikado (Mikado pheasant)
Tetraogallus caspius (Caspian snowcock)
Tetraogallus tibetanus (Tibetan snowcock)
Tragopan blythii (Blyth's tragopan)
Tragopan caboti (Cabot's tragopan)
Tragopan melanocephalus (Western tragopan)

Grus americana (Whooping crane)
Grus canadensis nesiotes (Cuban sandhill crane)
Grus canadensis pulla (Mississippi sandhill crane)
Grus japonensis (Red-crowned crane)
Grus leucogeranus (Siberian white crane)
Grus monacha (Hooded crane)
Grus nigricollis (Black-necked crane)
Grus vipio (White-naped crane)

Tricholimnas sylvestris (Lord Howe wood rail)

Rhynochetos jubatus (Kagu)

Chlamydotis undulata (Houbara bustard)
Choriotis nigriceps (Great Indian bustard)
Eupodotis bengalensis (Bengal florican)

Numenius borealis (Eskimo curlew)

Tringa guttifer (Spotted greenshank)

Larus relictus (Relict gull)

APPENDIX II

Megapodius freycinet abbotti
 (Abbott's scrub fowl)
Megapodius freycinet nicobariensis
 (Nicobar scrub fowl)

Lyrurus mlokosiewiczi (Caucasian black grouse)

Argusianus argus (Great argus pheasant)

Cyrtonyx montezumae mearnsi
 (Mearns' montezuma quail) -106
Cyrtonyx montezumae montezumae (Montezuma quail)
Francolinus ochropectus (Pale-bellied francolin)
Francolinus swierstrai (Swierstra's francolin)
Gallus sonneratii (Grey jungle fowl)
Ithaginis cruentus (Blood pheasant)

Pavo muticus (Green pea fowl)
Polyplectron bicalcaratum (Grey peacock-pheasant
Polyplectron germaini
 (Germain's peacock-pheasant)
Polyplectron malacense (Malay peacock-pheasant)

Turnix melanogaster (Black-breasted buttonquail)
Pedionomus torquatus (Plains wanderer)
Balearica regulorum (Southern crowned crane)

Crus canadensis pratensis (Florida sandhill cran

Gallirallus australis hectori (Eastern weka)

Otis tarda (Great bustard)

Numenius minutus (Little curlew)
Numenius tenuirostris (Slender-billed curlew)

Larus brunneicephalus (Brown-headed gull)

APPENDIX I

BIRDS (contd)

Caloenas nicobarica (Nicobar pigeon)
Ducula mindorensis (Mindoro imperial pigeon)

Amazona guildingii (St Vincent Amazon parrot)
Amazona imperialis (Imperial Amazon parrot)
Amazona leucocephala (Caribbean Amazon parrot)
Amazona pretrei pretrei (Red-spectacled Amazon parrot)
Amazona rhodocorytha (Red-crowned Amazon parrot)
Amazona versicolor (St Lucia Amazon parrot)
Amazona vinacea (Vinaceous Amazon parrot)
Amazona vittata (Red-fronted Amazon parrot)
Anodorhynchus glaucus (Glaucous macaw)
Anodorhynchus leari (Indigo macaw)
Aratinga guaruba (Golden conure)

Cyanopsitta spixii (Little blue macaw)
Cyanoramphus auriceps forbesi
 (Forbes' yellow-fronted parakeet)
Cyanoramphus novaezelandiae
 (Red-fronted parakeet)

Geopsittacus occidentalis (Night parrot)
Neophema chrysogaster (Orange-bellied parrot)

Pezoporus wallicus (Ground parrot)
Pionopsitta pileata (Brazilian pileated parrot)

Psephotus chrysopterygius (Golden-shouldered parrot)

Psephotus pulcherrimus p.e. (Paradise parrot)
Psittacula krameri echo (Mauritius parakeet)
Psittacus erithacus princeps (Principe grey parrot)
Pyrrhura cruentata (Blue-throated conure)
Rhynchopsitta pachyrhyncha (Thick-billed parrot)
Strigops habroptilus (Kakapo)

Tyto soumagnei (Madagascar owl)
Athene blewitti (Forest spotted owlet)
Ninox novaeseelandiae royana
 (Norfolk Island boobook owl)
Ninox squamipila natalis (Christmas Island hawk owl)
Otus gurneyi (Giant scops owl)
Ramphodon dohrnii (Hook billed hermit)
Pharomachrus mocinno costaricensis
 (Costa Rican resplendent quetzal)
Pharomachrus mocinno mocinno
 (Mexican resplendent quetzal)

Buceros bicornis homrai (Northern great pied hornbill)

Rhinoplax vigil (Helmeted hornbill)
Campephilus imperialis (Imperial woodpecker)
Dryocopus javensis richardsi
 (Tristram's white-bellied black woodpecker)

APPENDIX II

Gallicolumba luzonica (Bleeding heart pigeon)
Goura cristata (Blue crowned pigeon)
Goura scheepmakeri
 (Maroon-breasted crowned pigeon)
Goura victoria (Victoria crowned pigeon)

Cacatua (Kakatoe) tenuirostris
 (Slender-billed cockatoo)
Calyptorhynchus lathami (Glossy cockatoo)
Coracopsis nigra barklyi
 (Seychelles vasa parrot)
Cyanoliseus patagonus byroni
 (Greater Patagonian conure)

Cyanoramphus malherbi (Orange-fronted parakeet)

Cyanoramphus unicolor (Antipodes parakeet)
Eunymphicus cornutus (Horned parakeet)

Neophema splendida (Scarlet-chested parrot)
Opopsitta diophthalma coxeni
 (Coxen's double-eyed fig parrot)

Poicephalus robustus (Cape parrot)
Polytelis alexandrae (Princess parrot)
Probosciger aterrimus (Palm cockatoo)
Prosopeia personata (Masked shining parrot)

Psephotus (Northiella) haematogaster narethae
 (Little bluebonnet)

Tanygnathus lucionensis (Blue-naped parrot)

Gallirex porphyreolophus (Purple-crested turaco)
Tauraco corythaix (Knysna turaco)

Strigiformes spp* (Owls)

Aceros narcondami (Narcondam hornbill)
Buceros bicornis*(Great pied hornbill)

Buceros hydrocorax hydrocorax
 (Luzon rufous hornbill)
Buceros rhinoceros rhinoceros
 (Malayan rhinoceros hornbill)

Picus squamatus flavirostris
 (Western scaly-bellied green woodpecker)

APPENDIX I

BIRDS (contd)

Pitta kochi (Koch's pitta)
Cotinga maculata (Banded cotinga)
Xipholena atro-purpurea (White-winged cotinga)
Atrichornis clamosa (Noisy scrub-bird)

Dasyornis brachypterus longirostris
 (Western bristle bird)
Dasyornis broadbenti littoralis p.e.
 (Western rufous bristle bird)
Picathartes gymnocephalus (White-necked rock-fowl)
Picathartes oreas (Grey-necked rock-fowl)
Zosterops albogularis (White-breasted silver-eye)
Meliphaga cassidix (Helmeted honeyeater)
Spinus cucullatus (Red siskin)

Leucopsar rothschildi (Rothschild's mynah)

REPTILES

Batagur baska (Common batagur)
Geoclemys (=Damonia) hamiltonii (Black pond turtle)
Geoemyda(=Nicoria) tricarinata (Three-keeled land turtle)
Kachuga tecta tecta (Indian tent turtle)
Morenia ocellata (Burmese swamp turtle)
Terrapene coahuila (Aquatic box turtle)

Geochelone (=Testudo) elephantopus
 (Galapagos giant tortoise)
Geochelone (=Testudo) radiata (Radiated tortoise)
Geochelone (=Testudo) yniphora (Madagascar tortoise)
Gospherus flavomarginatus (Bolson tortoise)
Psammobates geometrica (Geometric tortoise)

Caretta caretta (Loggerhead turtle)
Chelonia mydas ** -107 (Green turtle)
Eretmochelys imbricata (Hawksbill turtle)
Lepidochelys kempii (Atlantic ridley turtle)
Lepidochelys olivacea (Olive ridley turtle)
Dermochelys coriacea (Leatherback turtle)
Lissemys punctata punctata (Indian soft-shelled turtle)
Trionyx ater (Black soft-shelled turtle)
Trionyx gangeticus (Ganges soft-shelled turtle)
Trionyx hurum (Peacock-marked soft-shelled turtle)
Trionyx nigricans (Dark soft-shelled turtle)

Pseudemydura umbrina (Western swamp turtle)

Alligator sinensis (Chinese alligator)
Caiman crocodilus apaporiensis (Rio Apaporis caiman)
Caiman latirostris (Broad-nosed caiman)
Melanosuchus niger (Black caiman)

Crocodylus acutus ** +210 (American crocodile)
Crocodylus cataphractus (Slender-snouted crocodile)
Crocodylus intermedius (Orinoco crocodile)
Crocodylus moreletii (Morelet's crocodile)
Crocodylus niloticus (Nile crocodile)
Crocodylus novaeguineae mindorensis (Mindoro crocodile)
Crocodylus palustris (Mugger crocodile)
Crocodylus porosus ** -108 (Saltwater crocodile)
Crocodylus rhombifer (Cuban crocodile)
Crocodylus siamensis (Siamese crocodile)
Osteolaemus tetraspis (Dwarf crocodile)
Tomistoma schlegelii (False gavial)

Gavialis gangeticus (Gavial)

Sphenodon punctatus (Tuatara)

APPENDIX II

Pitta brachyura nympha (Fairy pitta)

Rupicola peruviana (Andean cock-of-the-rock)
Rupicola rupicola (Guianan cock-of-the-rock)

Pseudochelidon sirintarae
 (White-eyed river martin)

Muscicapa ruecki (Rueck's blue flycatcher)

Psophodes nigrogularis (Western whipbird)

Spinus yarrellii (Yellow-faced siskin)
Emblema oculata (Red-eared firetail)
Paradisaeidae spp (Birds of paradise)

Clemmys muhlenbergi (Bog turtle)

Testudinidae spp * (Tortoises)

Cheloniidae spp * (Sea turtles)

Podocnemis spp (South American river turtles)

Alligatoridae spp* (Alligators)

Crocodylidae spp * (Crocodiles)

Cyrtodactylus serpensinsula (Serpent Is. gecko)
Phelsuma spp (Day geckos)
Paradelma orientalis (Queensland snake-lizard)

APPENDIX I

REPTILES (contd)

Varanus bengalensis (Bengal monitor)
Varanus flavescens (Yellow monitor)
Varanus griseus (Desert monitor)
Varanus komodoensis (Komodo dragon)

Acrantophis spp (Madagascar boas)
Bolyeria spp (Round I. boa)
Casarea spp (Keel-scaled boa)
Epicrates inornatus (Puerto Rican boa)
Epicrates subflavus (Jamaican boa)
Python molurus molurus (Indian python)
Sanzinia madagascariensis (Madagascar tree boa)

AMPHIBIANS

Andrias (=Megalobatrachus) davidianus
  (Chinese giant salamander)
Andrias (=Megalobatrachus) japonicus
  (Japanese giant salamander)

Bufo periglenes (Orange toad)
Bufo superciliaris (Cameroon toad)
Nectophrynoides spp (Viviparous African toads)
Atelopus varius zeteki (Zetek's golden frog)

FISH

Acipenser brevirostrum (Short nose sturgeon)

Scleropages formosus (Asian bony-tongue)
Coregonus alpenae (Long jaw cisco)

Chamistes cujus (Cui ni)
Probarbus jullieni (Ikan temoleh)

Pangasianodon gigas (Giant catfish)

Stizostedion vitreum glaucum (Blue wall eye)
Cynoscion macdonaldi (Totoaba)

APPENDIX II

Uromastyx spp (Spinytailed lizards)
Chamaeleo spp (Chameleons)
Amblyrhynchus cristatus (Galapagos marine iguana)
Conolophus spp (Land iguanas)
Cyclura spp (Ground iguanas)
Iguana spp (Iguanas)
Phrynosoma coronatum blainvillei
  (San Diego horned lizard)
Cnemidophorus hyperythrus (Orange-throated
  whiptail)
Crocodilurus lacertinus (Dragon lizardet)
Dracaena guianensis (Caiman lizard)
Tupinambis spp (Tegus)
Heloderma spp (Gila monster and beaded lizard)
Varanus spp* (Monitors)

Boidae spp* (Boas, pythons)

Cyclagras gigas (False cobra)
Elachistodon westermanni (Indian egg-eating snake)
Pseudoboa cloelia (Mussurana)
Thamnophis elegans hammondi
  (Two-striped garter snake)

Ambystoma dumerilii (Lake Patzcuaro salamander)
Ambystoma lermaensis (Lake Lerma salamander)
Ambystoma mexicanum (Axolotl)

Bufo retiformis (Sonoran green toad)

Acipenser fulvescens (Lake sturgeon)
Acipenser oxyrhynchus (Atlantic sturgeon)
Acipenser sturio (Common sturgeon)
Arapaima gigas (Arapaima)

Salmo chrysogaster (Mexican golden trout)
Stenodus leucichthys leucichthys (Beloribitsa)
Plagopterus argentissimus (Woundfin)
Ptychocheilus lucius (Colorado River squawfish)

Cynolebias constanciae (Pearlfish)
Cynolebias marmoratus (Ginger pearlfish)
Cynolebias minimus (Minute pearlfish)
Cynolebias opalescens (Opalescent pearlfish)
Cynolebias splendens (Splendid pearlfish)
Xiphophorus couchianus (Monterey platyfish)

Latimeria chalumnae (Coelacanth)
Neoceratodus forsteri (Australian lungfish)

APPENDIX I

MOLLUSCS

Conradilla caelata (Birdwing pearly mussel)
Dromus dromas (Dromedary pearly mussel)
Epioblasma (=Dysnomia) florentina curtisi
 (Curtis pearly mussel)
Epioblasma (=Dysnomia) florentina florentina
 (Yellow-blossom pearly mussel)
Epioblasma (=Dysnomia) sampsoni (Sampson's pearly mussel)
Epioblasma (=Dysnomia) sulcata perobliqua
 (White catspaw mussel)
Epioblasma (=Dysnomia) torulosa gubernaculum
 (Green blossom pearly mussel)

Epioblasma (=Dysnomia) torulosa torulosa
 (Tuberculed blossom pearly mussel)
Epioblasma (=Dysnomia) turgidula
 (Turgid blossom pearly mussel)
Epioblasma (=Dysnomia) walkeri
 (Brown blossom pearly mussel)
Fusconaia cuneolus (Fine-rayed pigtoe pearly mussel)
Fusconaia edgariana (Shiny pigtoe pearly mussel)

Lampsilis higginsi (Higgin's eye pearly mussel)
Lampsilis orbiculata orbiculata
 (Pink mucket pearly mussel)
Lampsilis satura (Plain pocketbook pearly mussel)
Lampsilis virescens (Alabama lamp pearly mussel)

Plethobasis cicatricosus (White warty back
 pearly mussel)
Plethobasis cooperianus (Orange-footed pimpleback)
Pleurobema plenum (Rough pigtoe pearly mussel)
Potamilus (=Proptera) capax (Fat pocketbook
 pearly mussel)
Quadrula intermedia (Cumberland monkey face
 pearly mussel)
Quadrula sparsa (Appalachian monkey face
 pearly mussel)
Toxolasma (=Carunculina) cylindrella
 (Pale Lilliput pearly mussel)
Unio (Megalonaias/?/) nickliniana
 (Nicklin's pearly mussel)
Unio (Lampsilis/?/) tampicoensis tecomatensis
 (Tampico pearly mussel)
Villosa (=Micromya) trabalis
 (Cumberland bean pearly mussel)

INSECTS

APPENDIX II

Mytilus chorus

Cyprogenia aberti (Edible pearly mussel)

Epioblasma (=Dysnomia) torulosa rangiana
 (Tan blossom pearly mussel)

Fusconaia subrotunda (Long solid mussel)
Lampsilis brevicula (Ozark lamp pearly mussel)

Lexingtonia dolabelloides
Pleorobema clava (Club pearly mussel)

Papustyla (=Papuina) pulcherrima
 (Manus I. tree snail)

Paraphanta spp +211 (New Zealand amber snail)

Coahuilix hubbsi ⎫
Cochliopina milleri
Durangonella coahuilae
Mexipyrgus carranzae
Mexipyrgus churinceanus
Mexipyrgus escobedae
Mexipyrgus lugoi   ⎬ snails
Mexipyrgus mojarralis
Mexipyrgus multilineatus
Mexithauma quadripaludium
Nymphophilus minckleyi
Paludiscala caramba   ⎭

Ornithoptera spp (sensu D'Abrera) ⎫
Trogonoptera spp (sensu D'Abrera) ⎬ birdwing butterfli
Troides spp (sensu D'Abrera)   ⎭

Parnassius apollo (Mountain apollo)

APPENDIX I

FLORA

Alocasia sanderana (an arum)
Alocasia zebrina (an arum)
Araucaria araucana ** +212 (Monkey-puzzle tree)

Caryocar costaricense

Gymnocarpos przewalskii (a pink)
Melandrium mongolicus (a pink)
Silene mongolica (a pink)
Stellaria pulvinata (a chickweed)

Fitzroya cupressoides (Fitzroy's cypress)
Pilgerodendron uviferum (a cypress)

Microcycas calocoma (Palma corcho)

Prepusa hookeriana (a gentian)

Santanea barbourii
Engelhardtia pterocarpa (a hickory)
Ammopiptanthus mongolicum
Gynometra hemitomophylla   } legumes
Platymiscium pleiostachyum
Pachigalia versicolor

Aloe albida (an aloe)
Aloe pillansii (an aloe)
Aloe polyphylla (Spiral aloe (Kharetsa))
Aloe thorncropftii (an aloe)
Aloe vossii (an aloe)

Lavoisiera itambana
Luarea longipetiola (a mahogany)
Artocarpus costaricensis (a mulberry)

Cattleya skinneri (White nun)
Cattleya trianae
Didiciea cunninghamii
Laelia jongheana
Laelia lobata   } orchids
Lycaste virginalis var alba
Peristeria elata (Holy ghost orchid)
Renanthera imschootiana (Red vanda ")
Vanda coerulea (Blue vanda orchid)

Abies guatemalensis (a fir)
Abies nebrodensis (a fir)
Podocarpus costalis   } yellow-woods
Podocarpus parlatorei

APPENDIX II

Pachypodium spp (Ghostman)

Panax quinquefolius ≠ 1 (American ginseng)
Araucaria araucana * -109 ≠ 2
(Monkey-puzzle tree)
Ceropegia spp (Rosary vines)
Frerea indica (a milkweed)
Byblis spp (Byblises)
All Cactaceae spp +213 (Cacti)
Rhipsalis spp

Cephalotus follicularis (Albany pitcher plant)
Chloanthaceae spp +214 (Lambstails)
Saussurea lappa ≠ 1 (Kuth, Costus)

Cyatheaceae spp ≠ 3 (Tree ferns)
Cycadaceae spp * (Cycads)

Dicksoniaceae spp ≠ 3 (Tree ferns)
Didiereaceae spp (Tree ferns)
Dioscorea deltoidea ≠ 1 (a yam)
Euphorbia spp -110 (Succulent euphorbias)
Quercus copeyensis ≠ 2 (Copey oak)
Anigozanthos spp (Kangaroo paws)
Macropidia fuliginosa (Black kangaroo paws)

Thermopsis mongolica
Aloe spp * (Aloes)

Swietenia humilis ≠ 2 (Mexican mahogany)
Verticordia spp
Orchidaceae spp * (Orchids)

Areca ipot   ⎫
Chrysalidocarpus decipiens   ⎪
Chrysalidocarpus lutescens (Butterfly palm)⎬ palms
Neodypsis decaryi   ⎪
Phoenix hanceana var. philippinensis   ⎪
Zalacca clemensiana   ⎭

Anacampseros spp (purslanes)
Cyclamen spp (Cyclamens)
Banksia spp (Banksias)

APPENDIX I

FLORA (contd)

Orothamnus zeyheri (Marsh rose)
Protea odorata (a protea)

Balmea stormae

Ribes sardoum (a currant)

Stangeria eriopus (a cycad)

Celtis aetnensis (a hackberry)

Welwitschia bainesii

Encephalartos spp (bread palm)
Hedychium philippinense (ginger lily)

APPENDIX II

Conospermum spp (Smoke bushes)
Dryandra formosa (Showy dryandra)
Dryandra polycephala

Xylomelum spp (Woody pears)

Boronia spp (Boronias)
Crowea spp (Croweas)
Geleznowia verrucosa

Solanum sylvestre

Stangeriaceae spp * (Cycads)

Basiloxylon excelsum ≠ 2

Pimelea physodes (Qualup bell)

Caryopteris mongolica

Welwitschiaceae spp *

Zamiaceae spp * (Cycads)

Guaiacum sanctum ≠ 2 (Tree of Life)

APPENDIX III

as at 28 June 1979

Interpretation:

1. Species included in this appendix are referred to:
   a) by the name of the species; or
   b) as being all of the species included in a higher taxon or designated part thereof

2. The abbreviation "spp." is used to denote all species of a higher taxon.

3. Other references to taxa higher than species are for the purpose of information or classification only.

4. An asterisk (*) placed against the name of a species or higher taxon indicates that one or more geographically separate populations, sub-species or species of that species or taxon are included in Appendix I and that these populations, sub-species or species are excluded from Appendix III.

5. Two asterisks (**) placed against the name of a species or higher taxon indicate that one or more geographically separate populations, sub-species or species of that species or taxon are included in Appendix II and that these populations, sub-species or species are excluded from Appendix III.

6. The name of the countries placed against the names of species or other taxa are those of the Parties submitting these species or taxa for inclusion in this appendix.

7. Any animal or plant, whether live or dead, of a species or other taxon listed in this appendix, is covered by the provisions of the Convention, as is any readily recognisable part or derivative thereof.

APPENDIX III

MAMMALS

Vampyrops lineatus (White-lined bat)	Uruguay
Bradypus griseus (Grey three-toed sloth)	Costa Rica
Choloepus hoffmanni (Hoffmann's sloth)	Costa Rica
Cabassous centralis (Costa Rican naked-tailed armadillo)	Costa Rica
Cabassous gymnurus (tatouay) (Uruguay naked-tailed armadillo)	Uruguay
Manis gigantea (Giant pangolin)	Ghana
Manis longicaudata (Long-tailed tree pangolin)	Ghana
Manis tricuspis (Tree pangolin)	Ghana
Epixerus ebii (Red-headed forest squirrel)	Ghana
Sciurus deppei (Deppe's squirrel)	Costa Rica
Anomalurus spp (Scaly-tailed squirrels)	Ghana
Idiurus spp (Pygmy scaly-tailed squirrels)	Ghana
Hystrix spp (Old World large porcupines)	Ghana
Coendou spinosus (Spiny tree porcupine)	Uruguay
Fennecus zerda (Fennec fox)	Tunisia
Bassaricyon gabbii (Bushy-tailed olingo)	Costa Rica
Bassariscus sumichrasti (Central American cacomistle)	Costa Rica
Nasua nasua solitaria (Uruguay coati)	Uruguay
Galictis allamandi (Allamand's grison)	Costa Rica
Mellivora capensis (Ratel)	Ghana, Botswana
Viverra civetta (African civet)	Botswana
Proteles cristatus (Aardwolf)	Botswana
Odobenus rosmarus (Walrus)	Canada
Hippopotamus amphibius (Hippopotamus)	Ghana
Hyemoschus aquaticus (Water chevrotain)	Ghana
Cervus elaphus barbarus (Barbary red deer)	Tunisia
Ammotragus lervia (Barbary sheep)	Tunisia
Antilope cervicapra (Blackbuck)	Nepal
Boocercus (Taurotragus) euryceros (Bongo)	Ghana
Bubalus bubalis (Asiatic buffalo)	Nepal
Damaliscus lunatus (Sassaby)	Ghana
Gazella dorcas (Dorcas gazelle)	Tunisia
Gazella gazella cuvieri (Edmi)	Tunisia
Gazella leptoceros (Rhim)	Tunisia
Hippotragus equinus (Roan antelope)	Ghana
Tetracerus quadricornis (Four-horned antelope)	Nepal
Tragelaphus spekei (Sitatunga)	Ghana

BIRDS

Rhea americana ** (Greater rhea)	Uruguay
Ardea goliath (Goliath heron)	Ghana
Bubulcus ibis (Cattle egret)	Ghana
Casmerodius albus (Great white egret)	Ghana
Egretta garzetta (Little egret)	Ghana
Ephippiorhynchus senegalensis (Saddlebill stork)	Ghana
Leptoptilos crumeniferus (Marabou stork)	Ghana
Hagedashia hagedash (Hadada ibis)	Ghana
Lampribis rara (Spot-breasted ibis)	Ghana
Threskiornis aethiopica (Sacred ibis)	Ghana
Anatidae spp * ** (Ducks, geese and swans)	Ghana
Crax rubra (Great curassow)	Costa Rica
Agelastes meleagrides (White-breasted guineafowl)	Ghana
Tragopan satyra (Satyr tragopan)	Nepal
Columbidae spp * ** (Doves, pigeons)	Ghana
Nesoenas mayeri (Pink pigeon)	Mauritius
Psittacidae spp * ** (Parrots)	Ghana
Ara ambigua (Great green macaw)	Costa Rica
Ara macao (Scarlet macaw)	Costa Rica
Musophagidae spp ** (Turacos)	Ghana
Bebrornis rodericanus (Rodriguez warbler)	Mauritius
Tchitrea (Terpsiphone) bourbonnensis (Mascarene paradise flycatcher)	Mauritius
Gubernatrix cristata (Yellow cardinal)	Uruguay
Xanthopsar flavus (Saffron-cowled blackbird)	Uruguay
Fringillidae spp * ** (Finches)	Ghana
Ploceidae spp (Weavers)	Ghana

APPENDIX III (contd)

REPTILES

Trionyx triunguis (Nile soft-shelled turtle)	Ghana
Pelomedusa subrufa (Helmeted turtle)	Ghana
Pelusios spp (Side-necked turtles)	Ghana

FLORA

Gnetum montanum	Nepal
Talauma hodgsonii (a magnolia)	Nepal
Meconopsis regia (a poppy)	Nepal
Podocarpus nerifolius (a yellow-weed)	Nepal
Tetracentron spp	Nepal

BIBLIOGRAPHY

Animal Life '73, The World Conservation Yearbook, ed. N. Sitwell. The Danbury Press, 1973

The World of Wildlife, ed. N. Sitwell. Hamlyn, London, 1977

All Heaven in a Rage; A study of importation of wild birds into the United Kingdom, T.P. Inskipp. Royal Society for the Protection of Birds, 1975

Airborne Birds; A further study of importation of wild birds into the United Kingdom, T.P. Inskipp and G.V. Thomas. Royal Society for the Protection of Birds, 1976

Porpoise, Dolphin and Small Whale Fisheries of the World, E. Mitchell. IUCN, Morges, 1975

Espécies da Fauna Brasileira Ameacadas de Extincao, ed. Academia Brasileira de Ciencias, 1972

Extinct and Vanishing Birds of the World, J.C. Greenway Jr. Dover, New York, 1967

The Red Book, Wildlife in Danger, J. Fisher, N. Simon and J. Vincent. Collins, London, 1969

Red Data Book Vol. 1 - Mammalia, compiled H.A. Goodwin and C.W. Holloway. IUCN, Morges, 1972

Red Data Book Vol. 2 - Aves, 2nd ed. part one, compiled W.B. King. IUCN, Morges, 1978

Red Data Book Vol. 3 - Amphibia and Reptilia, compiled R.E. Honegger. IUCN, Morges, 1975

The IUCN Plant Red Data Book, compiled G. Lucas and H. Synge. IUCN, Morges, 1978

The Turtle; A Natural History of Sea Turtles, A. Carr. Cassell, London, 1968

Vanishing Wild Animals of the World, R. Fitter. Midland Bank and Kaye & Ward Ltd, London, 1968

Red Data Book of USSR, USSR Ministry of Agriculture. Lesnaya Promyshlennost Publishers, Moscow, 1978

The Last of the Wild, E. Schumacher. Collins, London, 1968

White Gold, The Story of African Ivory, D. Wilson and P. Ayerst. Heinemann, London, 1976

Australian Endangered Species, D. Ovington. Cassell Australia Ltd, 1978

South African Red Data Book - Aves, W.R. Siegried, P.G.H. Frost, J. Cooper and A.S. Kemp, 1976

South African Red Data Book - Small Mammals, J.A.J. Meester, 1976

South African Red Data Book - Fishes, P.H. Skelton, 1977

South African Red Data Book - Large Mammals, J.D. Skinner, N. Fairall and J. du P. Bothma, 1977

South African Red Data Book - Reptiles and Amphibians, G.R. McLachlan, 1978

Rote Liste der Gefahrdeten Tiere und Pflanzen in der Bundesrepublik Deutschland, 1977

Whale Manual '78. Friends of the Earth Limited, London, 1978

Recent Advances in Primatology Vol. 2 - Conservation, ed. D.J. Chivers and W. Lane-Petter. Academic Press, London, 1978

Primate Utilization and Conservation, ed. G. Berman and D.G. Lindburg. John Wiley, New York, 1975

Man and Wildlife, L. Harrison Matthews. Croom Helm, London, 1975

Wildlife Crisis, H.R.H. The Prince Philip, Duke of Edinburgh, and J. Fisher. Hamish Hamilton, London, 1970

Animals in Danger, J. Sparks. Hamlyn, London, 1973

Last Survivors, Natural History of 48 Animals in Danger of Extinction, N. Simon and P. Geroudet. Patrick Stephens, London, 1970

This publication, edited by Jon Tinker, was researched and drafted by Tim Inskipp, Sue Wells and John Burton of TRAFFIC (a specialist group of the IUCN Survival Service Commission), with material from many TRAFFIC consultants.

Earthscan is grateful to World Wildlife Fund-US and the Fish and Wildlife Service of the US Department of the Interior for financial assistance towards the publication of this document. A Spanish edition in a duplicated format is available from Earthscan.

The opinions in this publication do not represent the views of IIED, TRAFFIC, FPS, IUCN, CITES, WWF-US, the US Fish and Wildlife Service, UNEP or any other agency.